Praise for
Possible

"Inspiring. Hopeful. Needed. *Possible: A Blueprint for Changing How We Change the World* is a beautiful road map for us all as we discover our role in bringing God's heart to the whole world."

> —LOUIE GIGLIO, pastor of Passion City Church and founder of the Passion Conference

"*Possible* is a beautiful, remarkable book. Stephan Bauman gives us a blueprint for changing the world that is light on superficialities and heavy on essentials. Whether you're a young activist discerning your path or a seasoned leader recalibrating for the road ahead, you'd do well to say a prayer and then start here."

> —JOSHUA DUBOIS, director of Values Partnerships and former executive director of the Office of Faith-Based and Neighborhood Partnerships at the White House

"This is an inspiring book! Written by the leader of one of the world's most effective relief and development organizations, it is full of stories that taught me and equipped me to be more effective in helping the way Jesus did."

> —DR. JOEL C. HUNTER, senior pastor of Northland, A Church Distributed

"There are many resources available on how to make a difference in the world. Stephan Bauman presents the most compelling blueprint I have read on how to do that. I wish I'd had this book as a reference and guide forty years ago!"

> —R. TIM ZIEMER, rear admiral, United States Navy (retired)

"Stephan Bauman is a visionary for what the people of God can do with a little faith. *Possible* doesn't just encourage us to believe in the impossible but gives us a blueprint for action. When so much can overwhelm us with what's wrong with the world, this book helps us act with, learn from, and come alongside those who are vulnerable. Weaving personal stories with practical application, this is an essential handbook to create a community of change makers."

> —JENNY YANG, vice president of Advocacy and Policy at World
> Relief and author of *Welcoming the Stranger*

"*Possible* is the book for everyone who wants to move beyond complacency to commitment and from doing little to truly changing the world. Lots of writers tell us that our world is a mess, but Stephan Bauman shows us how to fix it."

> —LEITH ANDERSON, president of the National Association
> of Evangelicals

"This is a book about not shrinking back from the challenges of the world but leaning into them with love, resolve, and inexplicable hope. It's about not doing easy things but doing lasting things. Stephan Bauman has rolled out something beautiful on the table. But it's not for us just to look at but to act upon. Part memoir, part manifesto—this book will challenge some of your assumptions and confirm others."

> —BOB GOFF, author of *Love Does*

"*Possible* is not just a blueprint for change; it's a cartography of courage. Stephan Bauman has personally challenged me to go beyond the safety of facile and distant engagement so pervasive in our age to the arduous but promising incarnational work of world changing. If you, like me, resist the cynicism that too often accompanies world changing, *Possible* calls you to leave the Shire with renewed hope."

—Rev. Gabriel Salguero, president of the National Latino
Evangelical Coalition

"In a world of poverty, suffering, and downright evil, Stephan Bauman calls us to live lives of hope, justice, and vision. He challenges us not to passively accept what is but to courageously rouse ourselves and our communities to make a difference in the world."

—Alec Hill, president of InterVarsity Christian Fellowship

"Stephan Bauman's new book, *Possible,* has all the marks of greatness. It avoids common pitfalls of many justice books that can either be overly optimistic or idealistic on one side or pessimistic and cynical on the other. This book is for people who still believe it is possible to change the world but want a deep and meaningful conversation on how to get there. Stephan has accomplished something special in this tight and compact treatise. It is passionately written, marked by Bauman's years of radically hopeful living. It is intellectual and deep yet remains accessible and inspiring. *Possible* is sure to spark your imagination and fire your passions."

—Ken Wytsma, founder of the Justice Conference and author
of *Pursuing Justice* and *The Grand Paradox*

"The weave and texture of *Possible* catapults this book to high levels of literary beauty, yet at the same time it emotionally and intellectually intertwines our lives with the most vulnerable of the world. Stephan Bauman's personal vulnerability connected with solid biblical, historical, psychological, and cross-cultural models make *Possible* a seminal book for our times."

—Jo Anne Lyon, general superintendent of the Wesleyan Church

"*Possible* invites us to take the first step toward living out God's purpose for our lives as agents of reconciliation and restoration in the world. Wonderfully accessible, user friendly, and faithfully grounded, Bauman's book challenges the status quo, answers the question 'what can I do?' and unleashes what's possible for ordinary people to address root causes of suffering and really change the world."

—DAVID BECKMANN, president of Bread for the World

"Stephan Bauman is a poet practitioner with the dirt of the world's biggest challenges under his fingernails. Many books point toward the world's problems, but few lay out reasonable solutions as *Possible* does."

—JUSTIN DILLON, founder and CEO of Made in a Free World

"I love this book! In *Possible,* Stephan Bauman helps us understand that if we want to responsibly steward 'our moment in history,' we need to turn our self-focused paradigm upside down. We need to recognize the 'enormous resilience, creativity, and unwavering hope' of those who suffer and then thank God for the privilege of coming alongside them as co-creators of solutions and change. Stephan and his wife, Belinda, have lived out the vision of *Possible.* When you read their story, I know you'll be as inspired and challenged as I have been."

—LYNNE HYBELS, Willow Creek Community Church

"A powerful combination of gripping stories, solid theology, and probing challenge. This book does not just call us to change the world; it convinces us that we can do it. A wonderful summons to do justice."

—RON SIDER, author of *Rich Christians in an Age of Hunger*
and Distinguished Professor of Theology, Holistic Ministry,
and Public Policy at Eastern University

POSSIBLE

POSSIBLE

A BLUEPRINT FOR CHANGING
HOW WE CHANGE THE WORLD

STEPHAN BAUMAN

MULTNOMAH
BOOKS

POSSIBLE
PUBLISHED BY MULTNOMAH BOOKS
12265 Oracle Boulevard, Suite 200
Colorado Springs, Colorado 80921

Hardcover ISBN 978-1-60142-582-9
eBook ISBN 978-1-60142-584-3

Published in the United States by WaterBrook Multnomah, an imprint of the Crown Publishing Group, a division of Random House LLC, New York, a Penguin Random House Company.

MULTNOMAH and its mountain colophon are registered trademarks of Random House LLC.

Library of Congress Cataloging-in-Publication Data
Bauman, Stephan.
   Possible : a blueprint for changing how we change the world / Stephan Bauman. — First Edition.
      pages cm
   ISBN 978-1-60142-582-9 — ISBN 978-1-60142-584-3 (electronic) 1. Change—Religious aspects—
Christianity. I. Title.
   BV4599.5.C44B38 2015
   261.8—dc23

                                        2014044431

Printed in the United States of America
2015—First Edition

10 9 8 7 6 5 4 3 2 1

SPECIAL SALES
Most WaterBrook Multnomah books are available at special quantity discounts when purchased in bulk by corporations, organizations, and special-interest groups. Custom imprinting or excerpting can also be done to fit special needs. For information, please e-mail SpecialMarkets@WaterBrookMultnomah.com or call 1-800-603-7051.

For Belinda, Joshua, and Caleb:
You are history in the hatching.

With God all things are possible.

—JESUS OF NAZARETH

contents

Part I: recovering our call

Part II: reframing the problem

Part III: remaking the world

Contents

POSSIBLE

Part I

Recovering Our Call

ONE

do we dare disturb the universe?

> Do you want to do something beautiful for
> God?... This is your chance.
> —MOTHER TERESA

During an otherwise normal worship service near Washington, DC, I received a text message I couldn't ignore. A rebel militia was wreaking havoc in the Democratic Republic of Congo, one of the world's most Christian countries yet also one of its poorest and most violent, especially for women and children. My wife, Belinda, was receiving similar messages on Facebook. Gunshots and mortar fire threatened the lives of people we loved.

I sat down to exchange a flurry of texts. Belinda sat down to cry. She was thinking about her friends in Congo. Only a few months before, Belinda knelt with Esperance, a victim of sexual violence, on the dusty concrete floor of a rural church, where they laughed and cried. "You remind me I am still human," Esperance said.

When you and I hear stories about violence, war, stolen girls, boy soldiers, or hungry children, we feel helpless, exasperated, sometimes even physically ill. When we learn about senseless poverty, brutal racism, mind-boggling violence, or preventable disease, we feel overwhelmed. We pray. Sometimes we give. But we struggle to do more.

Why?

Because we cannot change the world.

Or so we think.

A handful of years ago a friend from Indiana, Joe Johns, began to ask hard questions about conflict, faith, and peace in Congo. He and a Congolese pastor named Marcel began to help people see how local militias were turning neighbors against one another. Tensions between churches, they realized, mirrored tensions between tribes. So Marcel convened a group of fellow pastors to help them see where they were wrong. Some shed tears as they forgave one another. Others knelt and prayed together. All committed to developing a better future, making peace a priority, and mobilizing their communities to help people become peacemakers.

And mobilize they did.

Meanwhile, back home, Joe inspired his church to take on the impossible—saving Congo. His friends began to recruit their friends to help. Others gathered resources. Hundreds ran in their local half marathon to raise awareness. One group even rode bicycles across the country in a race to end Congo's suffering.

Across the country a rapper-poet and friend to Joe began to speak out on how tungsten, tin, and tantalum—all components in our cell phones and other electronics—help fuel the war in Congo, exploiting tribes and perpetuating violence against women. A few people from Bend, Oregon, also took the risk to talk about Congo, the impossible situation no one wanted to tackle. But they did anyway, their voices joining together to become a megaphone, a collective shout too loud to ignore.

A group of women from across the United States heard their appeal and traveled to Congo to meet those most affected by the conflict. Belinda joined their cause. They met ten women, including Esperance. All ten had been victims of violence and had overcome incredible odds to start businesses, provide for their children, and even forgive their perpetrators. They asked Belinda and the others to tell their stories so the world would know about "the vilest scramble for loot that ever disfigured the history of human conscience."[1] So one began to tell the world through art, another through digital portraits, and others through blogging.

And they haven't stopped since.

When Belinda learned Esperance had escaped the warring militias, she cried tears of joy. Esperance and her sisters found strength in each other, their communities, and their new friends across the world. Now they are helping other women—their "sisters"—some as young as fifteen, to heal from rape and rebuild their lives. Some are also working to mitigate future violence.

Today thousands of peacemakers are changing Congo, and their numbers continue to swell. With their friends from across the United States, they are waging peace to save Congo one village at a time.[2]

A poet and a blogger, a few warrior moms, two tenacious pastors, and a crew of volunteers offered their gifts, their strengths, their vulnerability, and their grit to inspire a sea of Congolese women, heroes on the front lines of suffering, to change their forgotten corner of the world in the Democratic Republic of Congo.

Can we change the world? I believe people like you will do extraordinary things when given the chance, turning some of the most entrenched, seemingly intractable situations of our day into something hopeful, something . . .

Possible.

I've seen it firsthand: students who took the time to help a child in Ghana learn how to overcome a life-threatening disease. A young couple who helped

5

a woman they'd just met to escape a war in Sierra Leone. The gutsy, over-worked doctor who helped a frightened mother deliver a baby girl only hours after an earthquake hit Haiti.

I believe "there are no *ordinary* people,"[3] only people who are bold enough to think they can save a life, or some corner of the world, and fierce enough to try.

seismic shift

I am convinced the world's suffering lingers not because people aren't willing to help. Faith, compassion, and justice stir the souls of many. They are blog-gers, technicians, musicians, entrepreneurs, artists, writers, nurses, electri-cians, rappers, moms, politicians, PhDs, lawyers, students, researchers, and doctors. They are you, and people like you—a groundswell of individuals who simply refuse to accept the world as it is. They *want* to give their lives to something more, something greater—something possible.

But we cannot change the world the way we used to. The vision of the past is insufficient to carry us into the future. While we honor those who have given their lives before us—their sacrifice, their ingenuity, and their perseverance—we are on the cusp of a seismic shift in how we bring change, moving from an era of a few extraordinary heroes to an era where tens of thousands, even millions, will effect change.

We face a crisis of vision, not will. I meet people every day who long to be part of meaningful change but experience disappointment instead. You may feel this way too. You may wonder if you can really make a difference, if you can genuinely impact the world. You understand the urgency, the gravity—real people, real lives, a billion hungry, twenty-seven million slaves[4]—and *why* we must do something. You may even understand *what can be done.*

But you may not know *how*.

Unfortunately the idea of changing the world has become rhetorical, superficial, and sometimes even cliché. What we call "change" may ring hollow or prove false. Efforts may be short-lived, paternalistic, or even harmful.

Many would-be activists succumb unwittingly to cynicism. A well-intentioned vision is oversold or gets reduced to a marketing slogan:

Overcome poverty by sponsoring a child.
Buy something "red" and eradicate AIDS.
Tweet "abolition" to end modern-day slavery.

We want to believe the world can be fixed that easily. But we know the challenges are far too complicated for easy solutions. And not only do quick solutions fall short, but they are also costly. Sometimes we do injustice to the very people we seek to help. We dabble with one issue, then shift our attention to another, or lose interest altogether, leaving our relationships shallow. We pursue versions of human progress void of local ownership, creativity, and perseverance.

We hurt ourselves too. We assume the answers—whatever they are—reside with us, because we're slow to recognize the deep wisdom and untapped potential of those who suffer. Our theology and practice remain tethered between false dichotomies of word and deed, sacred and secular, us and them.

God forgive us.

History is inviting us to join something deeper, something more, something beyond ourselves, where we boldly stare down the facts without dumbing down the issues, where we stay the course—from *impossibility* straight through to *possibility*.

Our tipping point is near. We can seize it—or miss it for a generation or more. With a better vision for how to change the world, you and I can reset how we engage and overcome some of the world's most desperate problems.

As outrageous as this might sound to you, this book tells how.

honest questions

Belinda and I didn't set out to change the world. In our twenties we left our rural hometown in Wisconsin for a six-month stint in West Africa, hoping to do some good while trying to find our calling. Having barely traveled, we were inexperienced and naive. Within months we were asked to lead a medical team into the bush. Villagers streamed to our makeshift clinic, some with mild infections, others with rare tumors, and one woman with a severe case of gangrene, her wound wrapped in chicken manure and banana leaves, the local remedy. Overwhelmed by the needs, the medical staff asked for our help. Belinda and I pulled guinea worms—a common, waterborne parasite— from the legs of children. I remember a boy letting a tear slip as I cleaned a wound near his eye. He was ashamed, perhaps for the pain he felt but more likely for needing help from me.

Days later I scavenged a used newspaper in Ghana's capital city of Accra. Its front page reported the World Health Organization had eradicated guinea worm from the planet.

I begged to differ.

Belinda and I had planned to volunteer in Africa for six months. We ended up staying for six years. I resigned my job in business back home, and Belinda resigned hers as a teacher. Africa became our home and justice our calling.

But Africa changed us more than we changed it. We left home with the hope of changing the world and came back wondering if it was even possible. We had answered the *why* question without adequately considering the *what* and especially the *how*. Well-intentioned as we were, if we learned anything, we learned by doing things the wrong way first. We went to Africa with answers and left with questions—honest questions regarding faith, culture, and what seemed like superficial solutions in light of a torrent of pain: *What is God's purpose in human suffering? What is my calling in light of this purpose? How can we create lasting change—change that meaningfully empowers those who suffer most? What must I learn from those I am seeking to serve? Who must I become? What is my appropriate role, given the rise in capacity in the majority world?*[5] Maybe you've asked similar questions.

Times have changed, and so have we. We've learned from our mistakes, the grace of friends, and the wisdom of those who suffer. There are good answers to your questions and mine, questions we'll explore together in the pages ahead.

In one of T. S. Eliot's poems, the character J. Alfred Prufrock asks, "Do I dare disturb the universe?"[6] But he queries not with courage or resolve but with cynicism and cowardice. Prufrock has given up, resigned to finish out his days without dreams or hope. But where Prufrock whimpers, you and I can declare, "With God we dare."

I am convinced that clear vision and thoughtful action will unleash us to do more and to do it better. There is a fork in the road for all of us. Faith or fear, courage or capitulation will determine our path. One is easy, the other difficult, but only one can create the lasting change we need most. As in every age, God calls his people to do the very thing we think we cannot do. Dallas Willard spoke of a coming age of unprecedented heroism, "a time for men and women to be heroic in faith."[7]

I believe that day has come.

overhaul

What if there was a better way to change the world, a vision of such pervasive change that only the language of reformation would suffice? God invites us to change the world. Biblical? *Yes.* Possible? *Yes.* But it will require an overhaul of how we understand our calling, a radical shift in how we see the problem, and an honest look at how we think, who we are, and how we live.

We cannot remain as we are. "Vision leaves our present situation indefensible," says Bill Hybels.[8]

Can we imagine a different future?

Envision tens of thousands, even millions, of people, whether young or old, rich or poor, super gifted or modestly talented, discovering their callings and employing their strengths to create meaningful, comprehensive, and lasting change in neighborhoods, villages, and cities.

Thus far, most of our efforts to change the world involve only a few—experts, clergy, and professionals—leaving the majority on the sidelines to serve marginally or to observe passively. Imagine instead a village or community that invites everyone, especially the most vulnerable, into the problem; that calls upon their diverse, resilient, and profound strengths; that co-creates solutions with those closest to the problem.

Imagine our global faith community, in all its expressions of worship, prayer, and study, focused first on those who are left out, those who suffer, those who are unable to experience the tangible love of God.

Much of our faith community is organized around ourselves, mainly our spiritual and social welfare. Out of our excess we devote a bit of time and resources to the vulnerable. But what if we were to flip this paradigm on its head and instead organize around God's love for the least first, where worship doesn't sidestep the world's suffering but includes them?

Consider a group of people so thoroughly captivated by truth, compassion, and justice that their words and actions spontaneously impact others to pursue the same.

Too often we offer compassion or "do justice"[9] merely to feel better about ourselves. We serve only if it's safe. We risk primarily for reward. Imagine, instead, a groundswell of people so thoroughly infused with the love of God that they risk their lives for others in uncommon ways.

I know people like this. Maybe you do too.

blueprint

This book proposes a set of universal principles—what I am calling blueprints—for anyone seeking to create and sustain change. Blueprints give just enough detail to help us visualize and build or arrive at something new. Think of a topographical map of a forest or mountain that shows the elevations, the likely terrains, the lakes. The geographical features are fixed, created years before, but the path you cut through the forest or over the mountains is personal and creative. Blueprints don't show everything, but they do point the way and infuse our creativity. The right blueprint can turn your life into a sacred adventure or quest, a journey that actually chooses you and changes you so completely you cannot resume your old life.[10]

There are three essential blueprints for us to discover:

1. The first is universal, archetypal, and invitational. It's God's divine blueprint for saving the world. It speaks to the purpose for

everything and why you are invited, by design, to join in. We'll explore several archetypal patterns of change and their implications for us today (chapters 1 and 2). And we'll grapple with, and reframe, age-old conundrums about faith and injustice (chapter 5).

2. The second is personal: how God has uniquely created, called, and designed you to participate in remaking the world. In chapter 3 we'll rethink who's called and why, dispelling some common myths. We will unpack the journey of calling, from the mountaintop experience through the valley of disappointment (chapter 4). Then we'll explore and expand the idea of creativity and our role in remaking the world (chapter 8).

3. The third is practical: what you must do to effect positive change, what the best way is to do it, and how to start. We'll explore a model for change to help you practically engage your community, church, neighborhood, or village (chapters 6 and 7). We'll also look at what it takes to multiply impact by investing in surprising agents of change (chapters 9 and 10). Finally I include two tools at the end of the book to help you practically apply these ideas to your context.

Throughout the book you will find suggestions to create your own blueprint for engaging and applying these principles to your life and the world. We will craft vision together, diagnose root issues, and map change. The ideas that follow are based on proven practices anchored in universal principles, so they will apply regardless of your context, and each will build upon the other.

If you are willing to accept this invitation, pick up a blank journal and across the first page write the word *Possible*. Unprecedented times call for exceptional people to do uncommon things. Let it begin with us.

a fellowship of dissidents

Sometimes the first step is the hardest. In the opening scene of the movie *The Fellowship of the Ring*, Sam Gamgee, a homegrown Hobbit who has never left his village, comes to the edge of the Shire to begin his unexpected journey. He says to Frodo, his Hobbit friend, "If I take one more step, it will be the farthest away from home I've ever been." Frodo replies, "Come on, Sam. Remember what Bilbo used to say: 'It's a dangerous business going out your door. You step onto the road, and if you don't keep your feet, there's no knowing where you might be swept off to.'"[11]

And so it is with us. The first step beyond the familiarity of home commits you to a journey that could falter or forever change the world and your life too. Sam Gamgee stepped into the "seeming void" and found "the rock" of faith.[12] I believe a rock is waiting there for you as well.

Years ago I took that first step, but I went kicking. I lived an ideal, almost clichéd life growing up in rural Wisconsin—*Green Acres* via rabbit ears on the family television, the Green Bay Packers on Sundays, and green bean casserole for the holidays. I played the drums in my father's wedding band, rang the altar-boy bells at church, and fell in love with the girl next-door.

After graduating from college, I began my days in a skyscraper cubicle with the *New York Times* and a cup of caffeine. And it was there that injustice split my world in two. For months the Serbian siege of Sarajevo, the longest in modern history, captured the world's attention. It caught mine too. I remember a 1993 headline that read: "Two lovers lie dead on the banks of Sarajevo's Miljacka River, locked in a final embrace." Bosko and Admira, both twenty-five, were shot by a sniper while trying to escape Sarajevo, the Bosnian capital, under siege. "They were shot at the same time, but he fell instantly and she was still alive," said a soldier who witnessed their deaths. "She crawled over and hugged him and they died like that, in each other's arms."[13]

In 1993 Belinda and I were also twenty-five. We were born just eight hours apart in the same small town in the same hospital and fell in love in high school, just like Bosko and Admira. For the first time I encountered war—viscerally somehow, even from the safety of my skyscraper. I could no longer dismiss someone else's injustice and suffering. Although a world away, Bosko and Admira felt up close and personal.

I vowed to do something.

At that time celebrities like Bob Geldof and Bono began talking about "stupid poverty," about suffering that just shouldn't be, about children dying from diseases the world had long known how to cure. The world witnessed the Ethiopian famine, courtesy of CNN. Nelson Mandela was rebuilding a nation torn and oppressed by racism. On the surface I ignored these currents, but privately, in the quiet corners of my busy days, I wondered if my faith was too small.

So I said a dangerous prayer: "God, if there is more, please show me."

Belinda suggested we volunteer in Africa, a dream she had nurtured for years, but I turned her down flat. When I finally said yes, I did so in stages. We committed to a few months at first, and then a few more, until we finally said yes for good. Belinda chose the "road less traveled"; I followed, and as Robert Frost said, it made all the difference.[14]

The groundswell we dream of requires more than a few people to say yes. If we can do this, you can too . . . and a couple hundred of your friends with you.

We need a generation to think big in order to inspire a fellowship of dissidents, innovators, and mavericks. When a Xhosa man was living out his twenty-seven-year prison term on Robben Island, off the coast of South Africa, he wasn't thinking about saving his country. He was doing something more difficult: forgiving his prison guard. When he walked free, he said, "I knew if I didn't leave my bitterness and hatred behind, I'd still be in prison."[15]

Twenty years later he invited his former prison guard to be his honored guest at his presidential inauguration. Nelson Mandela held back "a tide of violence"[16] in post-apartheid South Africa with radical forgiveness. Talk about change. Mandela said,

> Like slavery and apartheid, poverty is not natural. It is man-made and it can be overcome and eradicated by the actions of human beings. And overcoming poverty is not a gesture of charity. It is an act of justice. . . . Sometimes it falls upon a generation to be great. *You can be that great generation.*[17]

Mandela's words echo that of another dissident some two millennia earlier. Jesus, himself an unlikely candidate for bringing change, called the least likely people to change the world—many uneducated, all inexperienced, and all rough around the edges. His language to us is always "whosoever" or "if you believe" or "anyone who . . ."

Do we dare disturb the universe?

I suggest anything less than a full-throated *yes* is tantamount to turning our collective moral gaze away from what we know to be right, what we know to be biblical, and what we know to be possible.

speaking of faith

If you are new to faith, turned off for one reason or another, or merely an outsider looking in, I invite you to read on. Faith is at the heart of our conversation because the notion of saving the world demands answers to questions that are both epic and personal in scope.

A filmmaker friend who had all but thrown in the towel on faith traveled with me and a few others to Congo a few months after an upsurge in violence.

After meeting with several women who told us how they had forgiven their violent perpetrators, he made this stunning statement: "I don't believe in the God of the United States, but I believe in the God of Congo." My friend encountered people who spoke a profound message through their lives: "God is with us in our suffering, and that is enough. We believe." For him it took a journey into the heart of the world's suffering to glimpse the heart of a loving God.

I pray that you, too, discover the relentless God of the universe, not through shimmering stained glass, but instead through faces marred by suffering yet marked with unspeakable joy. No one is excluded from the quest to make a difference in the world. We need you now.

truth and dare

If you dare to disturb the status quo, then you are not afraid to seek the truth. You are probably already asking honest questions, such as these:

- Isn't it a bit arrogant to think I can really impact the world?
- What if I just don't have the stomach, let alone the courage, to take on suffering?
- Isn't God the only One who can save the world?

The following questions will help you grapple with the possibility of changing the world. They are designed to help you begin your journey toward meaningful change.

You may want to discuss these questions with your friends, family, small group, college class, book club, or church. Don't settle for pat answers, and don't give up on your big ideas and deepest hopes. Try not to overthink the questions; just give your honest response. If certain questions don't make sense to you, move on. They are meant merely to stimulate your thinking.

		Strongly Disagree	Disagree	Undecided	Agree	Strongly Agree
1	Needs should be understood first before trying to help.	❏	❏	❏	❏	■
2	Victims can help themselves.	❏	❏	■	❏	❏
3	Faith and justice belong together.	❏	■	❏	❏	❏
4	Everyone should change the world.	❏	■	❏	❏	❏
5	Simplifying the problem is important for people to engage.	❏	■	❏	❏	❏
6	It is important to be a voice for the voiceless.	❏	❏	■	❏	❏
7	It's best to do it right the first time.	❏	■	❏	❏	❏
8	Outsiders to the village, community, or neighborhood should be careful when offering help.	❏	❏	■	❏	❏
9	We will always have poverty in this life.	❏	❏	❏	❏	■
10	God wants us to help him save the world.	❏	❏	❏	❏	■

		Fairly Often	Sometimes	Almost Never
11	Over the life of a project, you see an increase in leadership by the people in the community, neighborhood, or village.	❑	❑	❑
12	You follow a learning process for understanding what works and what doesn't.	◼	❑	❑
13	You see resources coming from within the community over the life of a project or partnership.	❑	❑	❑
14	You are surprised by the root issues of injustice or poverty.	❑	❑	◼
15	You see people who are often considered victims speaking up for their community.	❑	◼	❑

After you've worked through these questions, consider journaling the reasons you are setting out on this journey, and list a few hopes as well. As you do, don't be afraid to dream.

Whoever you are, whatever your journey, I trust this book creates an event in your life marked by "before" and "after." I believe you will encounter God through this journey, because engaging suffering and injustice is a high calling, one that is close to the heart of God. What you do with your life matters—to you, to the world, and most of all to God.

TWO

the fierce urgency of now

Our lives begin to end the day we become
silent about things that matter.
—MARTIN LUTHER KING JR.

On October 31, 1517, a troubled monk reached for his mallet and nailed his complaints to the door of a church in Saxony. He described his years leading up to that day as "tortured and unprofitable," tortured because he began to "hate this God" who made it impossible for humanity to be saved, and unprofitable because he felt he had accomplished nothing of worth.[1] The swing of Luther's hammer against the medieval door of a Wittenberg church set fire to a continent. The world has never been the same.

What was Luther's complaint? He contested indulgences, the economic and spiritual extortion of peasants by the church. His vision? The recovery of an ancient and beautiful idea from the apostle Paul: "The just shall live by faith."[2] The mechanism? The printing press. Gutenberg's machines printed a quarter million copies of Luther's complaint. It went viral.[3]

Today we are experiencing a groundswell that could spark a new reformation. Our complaint? We won't tolerate a billion hungry people, 27 million enslaved kids, extreme poverty for millions, ethnic hatred, and the death of a child every twenty seconds from preventable disease.[4] The vision? *Faith shall live by justice.* If our faith is genuine, the world will know it by our deeds done in humility. Our printing press? The Internet.

In chapter 1, I suggested we are experiencing a seismic shift in how we change the world. I believe we face what Martin Luther King Jr. called "the fierce urgency of now,"[5] a window of time to comprehensively change how we change the world. If we succeed, we will experience something unprecedented: the overcoming of injustice at a pace never witnessed before in history. Such a groundswell would be largely nameless and faceless, a reformation of "deeds," not "creeds."[6] People are already rising up across the world, and not just the famous or the professional.

Consider the people who have changed the world—call them "reformers" and their legacy "reformation."[7] Few of them expected to change the course of history. Was it primarily the individual who shaped history, or did history shape the individual? We could argue both: influential people influence history, and history produces influential people. But reformations share common characteristics, or themes, beyond the exceptional people who lead them, no matter their context or cause. These themes are evident today, so much so that we owe it to subsequent generations to honestly ask ourselves if we are responsibly stewarding our moment in history. If we miss these, we may forfeit the reformation waiting in the wings.

Let's take a look at four themes that have profound implications today:

- Eras of significant change are marked by a recovery of truth.
- They are almost always sparked from the periphery.
- They are characterized by sacrificial love.
- They spread on the wings of innovation.

recovery of truth

Every significant era of change is marked by a recovery of essential truth, usually truth that releases people from some sort of injustice, evil, or oppression. For example, throughout history those in power have tended to reserve access to God for special people, such as clergy, saints, kings, or queens. Reformers in Luther's day upset the apple cart by seeking to allow *all* people, including peasants, to have access to God.

But before Luther, Jesus tackled the same problem. When Jesus unfurled a whip and drove out the temple moneychangers with fire in his eyes, he wasn't angry without reason. He had a singular goal in mind: to overturn a system that prevented common folk, the peasants of his day, from worshiping his Father.

Jesus didn't stop with the temple. In first-century Israel it was forbidden to mingle with sinners who were outside the Law. Fellowship with beggars, tax collectors, and prostitutes was a religious, social, and cultural taboo. The religious leaders didn't want good Jews mixing with riffraff around the dinner table. So when Jesus dined with prostitutes and fraternized with tax collectors, he was in effect saying to them, "Become a friend of God." To share a meal with someone is a declaration of peace, trust, fraternity, and forgiveness; the shared table symbolizes a shared life. Because Jesus was considered a prophet and a man of God, the sinners across the table received his gesture of friendship as divine approval. They were now acceptable to God.[8]

Jesus left his home in Galilee with a group of ragtag friends to change the world. Did he have it all figured out? I don't know. But he began with a complaint, an echo of another prophet years before: "Let my people go!"

Luther complained against the church of his day for awarding "salvation" to people with privilege, power, or pedigree. When he translated the Bible into German and wrote a few hymns to the tunes of popular folk songs, he offered all people, especially the peasants, direct and bold access to God, an idea considered an apostasy in his day. Luther complained and recovered truth along the way.

A few centuries earlier an abbey in Cluny, France—which for nearly five centuries was the largest church structure in the world—offered a new pilgrimage, the Compostela, to those who were left out of the religious services said to be "unequalled . . . in their splendour." Compostela sparked a reformation, a revival among the masses. Why? Because it offered "spiritual benefit to anyone who was capable of walking, hobbling, crawling, or finding friends who could carry them." It gave common people, not just the privileged few, access to holiness, to truth, to God himself. Compostela began with a complaint.[9]

So the question for us is this: What truth must be recovered today? We know the obvious ones: we cannot tolerate modern-day slavery, racism, people dying from hunger, or children fighting in wars. But what about the less obvious ones?

For too long change has been relegated to the professional. Those days are coming to an end. Everyone must care about the world, and everyone can contribute meaningfully. And, just as in Luther's day, today's "peasants" are being left out. Most people see the poor and vulnerable as victims without the capacity and potential to change their world. What if the vulnerable were empowered to lead their *own* change? Too often we seek to be a voice for the voiceless when we should be clearing the way for the voiceless to speak for themselves.

As with Luther and Jesus and Mandela and Bono, your willingness to step in, stand up, speak out—your courage to take action—begins with a protest. Something is not right in the world, and you can't walk by. Call it wrong. Call it injustice. Call it what you will, but it begins with a complaint. And complaints rightly pursued end in a recovery of truth.

from the periphery

The names we usually associate with change are famous ones: Martin Luther. Francis of Assisi and Clare. William Wilberforce. Mother Teresa. But they all began as unknowns, as unlikely heroes. In fact, the Reformation in the sixteenth century "sprang chiefly from the lower social strata"[10] with Luther, Knox, Cranmer, and Zwingli coming from peasant families. Even those of noble birth from the Counter Reformation and earlier movements, such as Ignatius of Loyola and Francis of Assisi, rejected their places in nobility in favor of monastic or peasant lifestyles.

Unlikely agents of change were important in the biblical narrative too. David, a shepherd boy, became king. Mary, a peasant teenager, gave birth to God incarnate. Jesus grew up in the sticks of a marginal country, hidden from a powerful empire. His ragtag group, uneducated and blue collar, launched a reformation upon which all other Christian movements are built.

If we were to canvass history, we would be surprised by how many of the world's greatest contributions were made by unlikely people. In 1852 a woman in rural Maine, Harriet Beecher Stowe, helped overturn slavery through her now-classic *Uncle Tom's Cabin*. She began writing an installment of stories because, as she said, "Every woman who can write will not be silent."[11] She raised her voice, to great controversy, by pleading with those who follow Jesus. When she met President Lincoln a decade later, he reportedly said, "So, you are the little woman who wrote that book that started this great war."[12]

Speaking of Abraham Lincoln, he was born in backwater Kentucky in a home without electricity, lost his mother when he was nine, failed at business, lost two children, and ultimately lost his life to an assassin.

But he saved a nation.

Today we are seeing an emergence of extraordinary people who are nameless and faceless to most of the world. They are surprising people. They are you and me.

Why does God recruit unlikely people? It seems God distributes wisdom disproportionately among surprising people in uncommon ways. The differentiator? Not pedigree, not fame, not necessarily expertise or skill, but humility. "My power is made perfect in weakness," said the apostle Paul:

God chose the foolish things of the world to shame the wise; God
chose the weak things of the world to shame the strong. He chose the
lowly things of this world and the despised things—and the things
that are not—to nullify the things that are.[13]

We often assume change starts from the center and flows to the edge. An important person, a powerful organization, or a titanic event triggers a movement, and things happen. Political campaigns gain momentum in capital cities. Actors become celebrities in Hollywood. Fashion trends begin in Paris or Milan. New business ventures are financed on Wall Street or London.

While culture may look for change in the city center, God specializes in change from the sticks. Reformations move from the edge to the epicenter, the margins to the middle, the periphery to the pinnacle. What we consider the fringes, God calls the center.

God designed it this way.

Can we imagine those who suffer bringing change to their world too? What if their change was so profound and lasting that it changed us?

In rural Cambodia reformation wears the skin of two Cambodian women who discovered a nineteen-year-old girl listless and lying beneath a house on stilts. Too ill to walk, she "lay down the whole time," was infected with HIV/AIDS, and "wanted to die because it was so difficult." Seven years before, at the age of twelve, her sister had led her from their home, telling her they were going to visit their aunt and uncle. When she questioned the way, her sister told her, "We don't want you to live with us anymore." Her sister took her to a brothel, where she was a sex slave until she escaped. Today she says this about her new friends:

> They shared with me about the love of God . . . and that he can give me life. That's why I'm still alive today. . . . They helped me learn to love myself again. And I know that God will not forsake me.[14]

In Los Angeles reformation wears the skin of my friend Micah Bournes. Micah grew up in a family of seven in a two-bedroom house in Long Beach. In college a few friends made fun of his poems. Now he travels the world, and when he speaks, a few thousand turn their heads.

In Congo reformation wears the skin of Madame Odile (pronounced "O-deel"). Her smile hides the suffering around her. Madame Odile gives her life for Congo's mothers, sisters, and daughters—many who have been raped in one of the world's most dangerous countries. She embraces a fifteen-year-old who escaped terror in the Virunga Forest. She clothes her. She treats her. She helps her family walk with her as she heals. And she works within the community to make it more secure so that one day the violence will stop.

If a rapper from LA can change a mind, if two friends from Cambodia can save a life, if a woman from Congo can change a village, why can't you and I?

Change begins at the periphery.

Shifting our expectations from the center to the periphery is essential if we are going to seize our moment in history. If we remain fixated on ourselves or on the "important" people, we will miss the reformation among us, the groundswell of unlikely people—some who have been written off as victims, as incapable, or—worse—as unworthy.

with sacrificial love

In the reformers and their movements, we also find a radical, sacrificial love. At the height of apartheid in South Africa, a crowd gathered to stone a white man who represented the perpetrator of oppression and violence for many years. Archbishop Desmond Tutu, compatriot of Nelson Mandela, was in the crowd. The archbishop knelt near the white man, who was now trembling, expecting to die. Then Tutu did something extraordinary: he reportedly stretched his body across the white man's. Without words he said, in essence, "If you kill this man, you kill me too and the hope for a better future for all of us."[15]

You may know people living out their faith in unprecedented ways like this. They inspire and humble us. These are ones

> Who stare down impossibility
> With tear-stained faces,
> Who wage war with vulnerable faith,
> Who laugh when devils cry,
> Who bolt their sister's hopes to wings that fly.[16]

But these people are still far too rare. What holds us back from sacrificial love, from greater impact? Could we be holding back a reformation as a result? Are we afraid?

"The paradoxical invitation of Jesus," said Jonathan Martin, "is to live defenseless . . . and yet live unafraid."[17] Living unafraid yet vulnerable has the potential to set the world on fire because faith is most attractive when it is least selfish. When onlookers to faith cannot clearly distinguish our motives, they shrink back. They wonder if any substantial difference exists between those who pursue God and those who don't.

And then someone comes along who's not afraid to call our bluff.

Dietrich Bonhoeffer, a German pastor, stood up to the Third Reich during World War II and died for both his faith and his involvement in a plot to assassinate Hitler. Bonhoeffer lived radically. He gave sacrificially. He was not afraid.

Referring to Martin Luther's decision to join a monastery early in his life, Bonhoeffer said his "attempt to flee . . . the world turned out to be subtle love for the world." Luther's decision to leave the safety of the monastery precipitated a series of events that eventually sparked a reformation. That choice prefigured Bonhoeffer's; he concluded that the only way to follow Jesus is by living deeply engaged in the world.[18]

Do we pursue God altruistically or for our own ends? Bonhoeffer spoke of grace as costly. In the end it cost him his life.

Martin Luther King Jr. is another example of courage. In his last speech, delivered the day before he died, King spoke about his absence of fear:

And then I got into Memphis. And some began to say the threats, or talk about the threats that were out. . . . Well, I don't know what will happen now. We've got some difficult days ahead. But it doesn't really matter with me now. Because I've been to the mountaintop. And I don't mind. Like anybody, I would like to live a long life. Longevity has its place. But I'm not concerned about that now. I just want to do God's will. And He's allowed me to go up to the mountain. And I've looked over. And I've seen the Promised Land. I may not get there with you. But I want you to know tonight, that we, as a people, will get to the Promised Land. And so I'm happy tonight. I'm not worried about anything. I'm not fearing any man. Mine eyes have seen the glory of the coming of the Lord.[19]

At the heart of every reformation were people who sacrificed greatly for love, for something higher than self. Some gave their lives, but many did not. But they all lived their lives *willing* to die. They were not afraid.

Several years ago I decided to leave behind easier, more popular messages about poverty and injustice and instead call people to live lives of radical obedience marked by sacrificial love. I asked students to choose one cause, one injustice, or one area of the world and commit their lives for five, ten, twenty, even thirty years, risking their comfort in their pursuit. Their response was clear: they wanted the real message, straight up, without gloss. Now I find people everywhere who want to give their lives to something meaningful. They long for something genuine and real, even if the cost is high.

Radical living marked by sacrificial love stands in stark contrast to the narcissism that characterizes much of the world. Holy, pure, and genuine lives given to something greater may do more to seize our moment in history than all our ideas, strategies, and activism put together.

on the wings of innovation

Innovation takes reformation to the masses. In the late fifteenth century, Johannes Gutenberg, a goldsmith, developed a printing system, using movable metal type, that could produce several hundred pages per day. Luther's complaints went viral the old-fashioned way—with ink and paper.

Other reformations witnessed innovations that may be considered less exciting, but they were no less important. The pilgrimage to Compostela in the eleventh century was an innovation. In Patrick's day Celtic monks copying the Bible fueled the conversion of Ireland. Luther's hymns brought theology to the masses. Wesley and Whitefield preached outdoors to the common people, a radical innovation in their day.

There are more. Benedict's Rule, Ignatius's *Spiritual Exercises,* the Westminster Confession, and many other seminal books and documents led to explosions in faith. The radio and tent meetings in the 1950s revolutionized American faith.

Today's unprecedented breakthroughs in communication technology set us apart in history. Never before has information been so accessible and our global village so connected. Our voices can be amplified across the planet through blogs, Pinterest, Instagram, Twitter, or Facebook. The explosion of innovation is changing the landscape of charity and justice.

The way we influence our networks—social, professional, and otherwise— may turn out to be the most important factor in converting our activism into reformation. Change is diffused through broad networks and institutions. For example, Wilberforce led the antislavery movement in Britain, but there would have been no movement without the Clapham community, a group of friends, many influential, who convinced Wilberforce to join their pursuit against injustice. Even Luther was surrounded by an important group of influencers across northern Germany. James Davison Hunter said,

> The key actor in history is *not* the individual genius but rather the
> network and the new institutions that arise out of that network. This
> is where the stuff of culture and cultural change is produced.[20]

This is not to undermine or undersell the importance of charismatic figures like Luther, Calvin, or Wilberforce. But their courage and charisma, however, cannot be understood apart from a network of similarly oriented people.

With the wealth of technology available to us today, we are left without excuse. There has never been a period in history where so many people are exposed to so much opportunity.

you say you want a reformation

If you believe we need to desperately change how we change the world, and if you sense we are experiencing an unprecedented moment in history, then where do we start?

Just as with Luther and Jesus and Bono and so many others: *with a complaint.*

Why not write your name in the annals of history by objecting to the status quo? Begin by journaling a few lines, even a poem. Then let your complaint become a prayer—the passionate, deeply honest kind—to galvanize your courage. Your courage will foster commitment, and your commitment will become the foundation for action. When done well, a complaint can move mountains.

Complaints can be spontaneous, but they can also follow time-honored patterns. When you set out to craft one, consider the following:

- *Begin with what bothers you.* Is it hunger? poverty? violence? a certain place in the world? your city? Who is not in the conversation? Who should be? What wrong attitudes or assumptions must be challenged? What leads you to say, "This simply cannot be"?
- *Choose one issue and immerse yourself.* Ask the hard questions, read, watch TED talks on the topic, follow your heroes on Twitter.

- *Consider writing out your complaint.* For example, years ago just after visiting Haiti, I came across the story of a woman who had to choose which child to feed, her son or her daughter, because she didn't have enough to feed both. I complained by writing a poetic version of this sentiment in my journal: "I cannot tolerate a world where moms are forced to choose which child to feed."

- *Turn your complaint into a postmodern lament.* There is an ancient blueprint for complaining in the Bible, especially in Psalms, called a *lament.* Laments are prayers for help in times of trouble, but they are often characterized as redemptive because they do more than just complain. The language of lament is anchored in hope, born out of faith with confidence in a God who is not standing idly by. Consider the end of Psalm 10, for example:

You hear, O Lord, the desire of the afflicted;
> you encourage them, and you listen to their cry,
defending the fatherless and the oppressed,
> in order that man, who is of the earth, may terrify no more.

Sometimes laments begin with an introduction, or call. Other times they launch into a full-on complaint: *God, why don't you hear me? Why do the innocent suffer? Why don't you put an end to the evil?* When we heed the psalmist and pour out our hearts before God,[21] we release our deepest emotions, making way for forgiveness and healing. When we trust God in the midst of suffering, he converts our anger into love. And when we love, we discover what God *will* do and how we might join him. In a very real sense our complaints become windows for meaning-filled action.

When I was twenty-five, someone told me to pick one thing that concerned me and pray about it for thirty days. He told me I would be stunned by what happened. The war in the Balkans was raging then, so I began to pray for the people I was encountering in the newspaper each morning. My prayers informed my complaint, my complaint turned into a lament, and my lament spurred me to action. A year later I was seeking UN approval to bring medical supplies into Belgrade. The journey in between was nothing short of miraculous. Trust me, I was the least likely candidate for such an undertaking. It was my complaint that put me there. I am sure of it.

You and I have a chance to bend history's arc toward justice.[22] We can foster a movement, a lament that could echo around the world. But it will be the hardest thing we'll ever do. If we aggressively pursue truth, if we are willing to sacrifice, if we look for wisdom from those on the periphery, we have the potential to shock the world from its apathy.

Urgent? Fierce? Now?

Yes.

THREE

there's more to you

than you know

Be who God meant you to be and you will
set the world on fire.
— CATHERINE OF SIENA

To change the world, we must first change ourselves.

Underneath a canopy of stars near one of Rwanda's pristine lakes, where fish eagles dive-bomb tilapia and hippos lurk at the waterline, my son Joshua asked, "Do you ever feel stuck to the earth?"

Joshua, who was thirteen at the time, has a poetic flare, so I knew he wasn't talking about gravity. We had been visiting villages in Burundi and Rwanda for several days. I knew he was inspired by the resilient people he had met but also overwhelmed by the challenges they faced. Joshua had never seen suffering like this. He wished he could do more.

"Yes, I think so, Joshua," I said. "Why do you feel that way?"

"Because I think God has put something big inside me, but I don't know what it is." His voice quavered as he spoke.

Perhaps you too are beginning to experience an awakening of something new. Or maybe you've always felt there is something untapped deep down inside. I believe our longings for something more point to something greater, something important.

We do well to listen to them.

C. S. Lewis, author of *Mere Christianity* and creator of Narnia, spoke of his longings as divine "arrows of Joy [that] had been shot [at him] ever since childhood."[1] They were moments of such overwhelming desire they forced him to consider another reality. But Lewis, then a committed atheist, struggled to reconcile his yearning with his skepticism. In September 1931, during an evening walk along Addison's Path in Oxford, J. R. R. Tolkien, creator of The Lord of the Rings trilogy, made an appeal to Lewis. He asked him to approach the idea of Christ first with his imagination and then, after having done so, to put it to rational test. Tolkien was taking a cue from the prominent seventeenth-century scientist and apologist Blaise Pascal when he cautioned against an overreliance on reason. Instead, Pascal said, we should "make people wish that it were true, having caught sight of the rich and satisfying vision of the reality it offered. Once such a desire was implanted within the human heart, the human mind would eventually catch up."[2]

While Lewis rejected Christianity *intellectually*, he had failed to understand its significance *imaginatively*. Tolkien offered Lewis a new pathway to God, a means by which to bring together his intuition and reason. Just days after his conversation with Tolkien, Lewis, in his own words, "passed over" into belief in Christ.[3]

Through Narnia, Lewis helped twentieth-century readers imagine a God of outrageous love, a God who relentlessly pursues his people, inviting them to join him in returning goodness and joy to a once-happy world. With *Mere Christianity* and other works, Lewis provided the theological rationale for the truth of Narnia: imagination first, then intellect. Lewis's "argument from desire" is an apologetic for the existence of heaven and even God himself.[4]

What if our desire to engage the world is also a divine arrow, inviting us to live more fruitful lives here and now? And what if we were to apply this same approach—discovering first with imagination and then proving through logic—to changing the world?

In Tolkien's *The Hobbit,* Gandalf says of Bilbo, "There is a lot more in him than you guess, and a deal more than he has any idea of himself."[5] So often we approach personal change by analyzing our deficits, or shortcomings, during seasons of introspection. Yet sometimes the greatest leap forward begins by first embracing what we already have, by accepting the glorious grace already etched in our souls.

Do you, like my son Joshua, ever feel stuck to this earth? Do your longings ever convince you there must be something more?

The psalmist said, "Delight yourself in the LORD; and He will give you the desires of your heart."[6] "We are God's masterpiece [*poems* in the original text]," Paul said, "created in Christ Jesus to do good works, which God prepared in advance for us to do."[7] Jesus said, "You did not choose me, but I chose you and appointed you to go and bear fruit—fruit that will last. Then the Father will give you whatever you ask in my name."[8]

The promise given to Abraham through a billion stars is meant for Joshua and you too. We are all like Bilbo: too afraid to believe there is something more but not ready to give in to our doubts and still courageous enough to risk our comfort for something greater. The God of fingerprints and snowflakes and galaxies has prepared something unique and specific for you. I'll stake my life on it.

There is more to you than you know.

who can tell me who i am?

In a poignant moment in one of Shakespeare's well-known plays, King Lear asks, "Who . . . can tell me who I am?"[9] Ironically, the Fool in the play answers by saying the king is only Lear's shadow.

Why is it so easy to leave the better parts of ourselves undiscovered?

Our society tends to define us by a fraction of our full capacity and identity, by our "shadows," rather than by who we really are. We default to a person's utility, his or her profession—a driver, a teacher, a carpenter—conflating identity with purpose. Worse, sometimes we define people by their least common denominator—poor, rich, white, black, old, juvenile, and so on.

Take my wife, Belinda, for example. She spends most of her days driving our kids here and there and cheering them on in their adolescent dreams, however mundane or magical. She finds time to stay connected too. Our kids say, "Mommy is addicted to Facebook just like we are addicted to Minecraft."

But Belinda also writes about the plight of women. She speaks regularly to large groups of people and makes them cry. She has a penchant for connecting with well-known people too. She chatted with Laura Bush once and laughed with President Obama twice. I've never seen anyone better able to touch a person's heart so quickly with so few words. She embodies empathy and exudes trust.

Who is Belinda *really*? Most would say she is a stay-at-home mom, a teacher, or maybe the wife of a CEO. But she is also an advocate for the world's suffering. She's a prophet, of sorts, to those thirsty to change the world. She paints pictures with words, heals hearts with empathy, and midwifes dreams with prayer.

Or consider Mr. Chey, who lives in rural Cambodia, one of the poorest countries in Asia. Several years ago Chey was "searching for something to erase the guilt he lived under." Several fellow villagers spoke to him about the hope they had discovered by following Jesus. Chey chose to follow too. Now a lay pastor of an indigenous cell church movement that serves thousands, Chey leads others to the same hope he discovered. He spends his extra time encouraging those living with HIV/AIDS. Chey is making a difference. In a nearby village the elders said that since "Jesus came to our village, our children are healthier, the sick are being cared for, and people are getting along with each other."[10]

Who is Mr. Chey then? Many would see only a poor man struggling to make ends meet. Some might call him vulnerable. But Mr. Chey is much more than that. He's a leader in his community. He is a social entrepreneur and an activist. Many contemplate strategies to help the millions suffering from HIV/AIDS, but Chey puts feet to his faith. He helps his neighbors care for those suffering with the disease.

Labels put on others are bad enough, but there's a deeper problem: most people don't live beyond their labels. According to Harvard psychologist Ellen Langer, a person labeled "secretary" performs only secretarial duties, never more. A child shrinks from responsibility because, after all, she's been told she's "only a kid." A grandfather caves in to the stigma associated with being "elderly" and begins to contribute less to society. In the extreme, according to Langer, "When one is rendered helpless by others, one gives up."[11]

In short, when people are categorized, it's hard for them to rise above the label.

All this makes it difficult for us to believe the words of Jesus: "I chose you to bear fruit—fruit that will last."[12] We may *say* we believe Jesus, but in our day-to-day lives, we chalk up his words to rhetoric or sentiment, slinking back behind our labels.

But the Creator of the universe chose us when we were without utility, when we had nothing to offer. He chose us because we belong to him. He chose us to change us and to change the world through us. We bear his image, the *Imago Dei,* his likeness—all of us. Our identity, capacity, and function are anchored in God himself. And this likeness—God's vision, character, and potential—can inspire our thoughts, our words, our passions, our actions. It can drive our motives. It can permeate everything we do.

I talk to people all the time who say, "What can I do? I am *just* a businessman [artist, skater, teenager, musician]." "Just a . . ."—what a horrible way to describe ourselves The truth is that, like King Lear, our titles and labels are mere shadows of who we really are. Just as Tolkien challenged Lewis, we can muster the courage to imagine *first* what we might become before rationalizing away our potential, along with the possibilities that follow.

what happens when we say yes

Amalie is an artist in Florida. She awakens people with chalk and acrylic. Injustice is familiar to Amalie. She was assaulted while walking home one night and has lived with the pain ever since. She splashes justice onto canvas in the midst of the world's suffering—their suffering, their joy, and hers too. A decade ago Amalie took a radical step of obedience: she left home with a few artist friends for rural villages in Guatemala and later Africa. Together they call upon communities "to do something beautiful for God"[13] by painting murals in public places. As kids, moms, and dads paint their collective stories, Amalie comes alongside, around, and in between with color, brush, and laughter to weave in a landscape, to strengthen a smile, to add perspective, contrast, and always a beam of light. An ordinary wall in an otherwise ordinary village becomes an open canvas. Common people tell their stories and experience a new day.

Something beautiful begins.

Scott sells medical supplies in Bend, Oregon. He and his wife, Darcy, wanted to travel the world, but they brought the world home instead: they adopted two Congolese boys. On a bitterly cold Oregon day at the Justice Conference, Scott stood when I called for entrepreneurs to follow Jesus by taking on the great injustices of the world. Just two years later he launched a mobile app called Forgo, which calls people to *forgo* a meal or coffee or party and instead give to a just cause like Congo. Scott boldly merged his professional career with a calling to change the world.

Mike is a businessman from Minneapolis. During a Bible study one evening, a friend named Steve mentioned he was traveling to Mafinga, Tanzania, on business. Surprised, Mike told Steve he had just been in Mafinga to visit a construction project. Steve's business in Tanzania grows pyrethrum, a flower that looks like a daisy but, when dried and processed, becomes the world's greenest pesticide. Since it grows in volcanic soils at high elevations, the mountains near Chitipa, Malawi, are a perfect match. Mike's church had long worked in the Chitipa area with local farmers and pastors. His goal? A market-driven, sustainable agribusiness with better-than-fair economic solutions for the poor. Today more than seven hundred families grow pyrethrum and sell it for processing and export. Their lives are changing as a result.

Three people dared to leap, to believe the God of the universe called them to become something more, to do something extraordinary, to spark something new. They are living astonishing lives.

the myth about calling

But are Amalie, Mike, and Scott really so different from us?

The idea of a specific, unique calling for every person is controversial. Some say God reserves calling, or election, for only a few and certainly not all. Others are more pragmatic. They say such ideas raise false hopes that cannot be fulfilled.

But Jesus disagreed. He prayed *not* just for his disciples but "for those who will believe in me through their message."[14]

And he appealed to everyone to do great things:

Very truly I tell you, *whoever believes in me* will do the works I have been doing, and they will do even greater things than these, because I am going to the Father. And I will do whatever you ask in my name, so that the Father may be glorified in the Son. You may ask me for anything in my name, and I will do it.[15]

In the New Testament the word *whoever* (*whosoever* in older translations) is used more than a hundred times by Jesus, Paul, and others: "Whoever believes . . . ," "Whoever wants to be my disciple . . . ," "Whoever acknowledges me . . . ," "Whoever does these things . . . ," "Whoever aspires . . ." With the constant use of this gender-neutral pronoun, God invites *all*. Everyone. Us. Them. You. Me.

No one is left out. Everyone is called.

Why? Because calling is essential to the nature and character of God. His unconditional love necessitates an invitation to all who bear his image. He is committed to our becoming, our formation, but also to our vocation, our purpose.

The idea of calling in the Bible is nuanced, however. Some texts refer to our identity, our calling as the people of God, while others refer to our calling as a vocation, even specific responsibilities and tasks. Os Guinness distinguishes between *primary* and *secondary* callings. "First and foremost we are called to Someone," he says, namely God. This is our primary calling. Our secondary calling is to specific tasks and responsibilities. According to Guinness, we must "never split the primary call . . . from the secondary call," and the first must drive the second.[16]

This nuance regarding calling prioritizes our *identity,* who we are, versus our *utility,* what we do. Calling is not a class system, split between sacred and secular, clergy and laity. The sixteenth-century Reformation took care of this heresy even though we often slip back into it. Martin Luther proclaimed all forms of work as honorable, even saying "when a father . . . washes diapers . . . God, with all his angels and creatures, is smiling."[17] "To be a farmer, a craftsman, or an artist [is] just as much a vocation, a calling from God, as to be a preacher," said Tim Keller. He added:

> If the Holy Spirit is not only a preacher that convicts people of sin and grace . . . but also a gardener, an artist, and an investor in creation who renews the material world, it cannot be more spiritual and God-honoring to be a preacher than to be a farmer, artist, or banker.[18]

Despite widely accepted theological notions like the priesthood of all believers,[19] we still look to the few—call them saints or celebrities or pastors or professionals—as specially chosen people "elected" by God. Our practical theology needs an overhaul. Millions of people are held back because they really don't believe they are called. A liberation is waiting to happen.

We speak of setting the oppressed free, of proclaiming freedom for the captives, or releasing prisoners from darkness[20] without realizing that we need deliverance from our own oppression. We are too prone to narcissism, self-absorption, and insecurity. Simple admission, confession, and repentance can radically liberate us from ourselves so we are free to receive and pursue a higher calling. Such a transformation can be absolutely life changing.

Bonhoeffer wrote about the burden of self as more difficult, more onerous to bear, than the burden to serve others. This seems like a paradox. How can this be? Most of what we encounter in our consumer society is some version of the idea that if you serve yourself, you will be happy. But Jesus said the opposite: give yourself away, and you will be fulfilled. Recent research says that people who pursue "extrinsic goals," which include helping others, are happier than those who don't.[21] Seems as though Jesus's ancient claim is being substantiated.

It's time we dispel the myth that calling is for only a select few. Dismantling this myth will release millions of people to meaningfully participate in changing the world. The implications are paradigm shifting, far reaching, and profound.

The idea that everyone has a unique calling is captivating. But seeking that calling is for those who are willing to sacrifice for a vision higher than self and to fight for it over a lifetime. Sounds difficult, I know. But supernatural grace is waiting for those willing to step into the unknown. I've tasted it. You can too.

God has prepared a unique destiny for everyone. Rich and poor. Clergy and laity. Young and old. Whether we choose to accept it is not God's problem but ours.

the world is ours to save

If we are all called, then what is our role in saving the world?

An American gynecologist managed to get to Port-au-Prince within hours of the 2010 earthquake in Haiti, tagging along with his orthopedic surgeon friend. I admit, when I met Dr. OB-GYN, I naively thought, *This is no place for a baby doctor.* To my surprise he delivered an infant girl within a few days of the quake. Her mother, Thamar, wearing a full leg cast due to a broken femur, had lost her two-year-old son when her home collapsed. Amid her overwhelming grief, she named her newborn daughter Jesula. Its meaning? "God is with us."

In the middle of untold suffering, Thamar chose to name her daughter after God. Despite the death of her son, she placed the Father of Life in the middle of her tragedy. Thamar helped me discover a God fully present at ground zero, tangibly alive, incarnated in human skin, breathing new life, consoling grief, and healing bones. As the world watched the tragedy unfold on CNN—asking, "Where is God in such pain?"—God was effectively calling back, "I am right here, among the suffering, bringing new life, even in death."

People sometimes say, "Saving the world is God's business, not ours." In fact, some may think that trying to save the world is too liberal, too proud, or too social. We might all be called, but who are we to think we can save the world?

Let's be clear. Without God we are all lost. When it comes to redemption, it's all God and only God. We cannot save ourselves.

But too often we shirk our responsibility. From a theological perspective, we don't want to pridefully impose our inability upon an all-powerful God. That is understandable.

But are we not invited to *join God* in saving the world? Doesn't Christ work in and through us? Christ alive in our hands and feet? Christ present in our tears and prayers?

This is not a new idea but rather an ancient, biblical, and thoroughly orthodox one. Jesus said we would do "greater things" than he did. Paul said God is "making his appeal" through us. We are his "ambassadors," participating with Christ in bringing his salvation to the world.[22] Christ is complete when joined together with us, the church, to become the *Totus Christus,* the *total* Christ. We are, in effect, the ongoing incarnation, says Jürgen Molt-mann,[23] God's hands and feet on the earth. "Every Christian is to become a little Christ," said Lewis. "The whole purpose of becoming a Christian is simply nothing else."[24] Even earlier, Augustine said:

> Let us rejoice then and give thanks that we have become not only
> Christians, but Christ himself. Do you understand and grasp . . .
> God's grace toward us? Marvel and rejoice: *we have become Christ.*
> For if he is the head, we are the members; he and we together are . . .
> the fullness of Christ.[25]

Rather than a contradiction or some poetic paradox, when Jesus said, "Apart from me you can do nothing" and "Ask whatever you wish, and it will be given you,"[26] wasn't he effectively saying, "Apart from me you can do nothing, but with me you can do anything"? N. T. Wright summarized "the work of salvation" this way: "Salvation, in its fullest sense, is about whole human beings, not merely souls; about the present, not simply the future; and about what God does *through* us, not merely what God does *in and for* us." He continued:

> When God saves people in this life, such people are designed to be a
> sign and foretaste of what God wants to do for the entire cosmos. . . .
> What's more, such people are not just to be a sign and foretaste of that
> ultimate salvation; they are to be part *of the means* by which God
> makes this happen in both the present and the future. . . .
>
> In our humility and brokenness, we tend to emphasize our
> humanness. We are indeed limited, even frail, and prone to injury
> rather than love. Sin and brokenness casts a great shadow. But have we

missed the profound mystery of the Gospel amidst our weakness? God wants to live and breathe in us, and through us, in ways far beyond our imagination. We are the *means* by which God brings salvation here, now, and into the future.[27]

Our words, *his* words. Our actions, *his*. Our thoughts, the thoughts of Christ. In effect, "Christ becomes what we are . . . so we may become what he is," wrote William Wrede.[28] What if suffering tarries not because God isn't willing or ready but because he's waiting—waiting for us to join him, the living God, here on earth?

If the many, rather than the few, were to rise in faith to take hold of their divine call, if we were to overcome our skepticism and fear, wouldn't we have the beginnings of a reformation?

I think a Haitian woman named Thamar, her daughter Jesula, and an American gynecologist would absolutely, unequivocally say *yes*.

the extreme middle

But maybe your concerns are less theological and more about your capacity to meaningfully contribute to saving the world. Sometimes we try so hard to save the world in our own strength that we find ourselves burned out and bitter.

Belinda and I led several humanitarian missions during the Balkan wars in the mid-1990s. The suffering of Bosnians, Croatians, and Kosovars was overwhelming. Photos and images of war filled newspapers and television screens for several years. I remember standing at the freshly dug grave of a two-year-old girl in Kosovo, thinking, *God, why?*

Getting approval from the United Nations to bring medical supplies into the Balkans was tantamount to moving mountains with a garden shovel.

Long days and late nights left us exhausted. A friend noticed my frenetic pace. He pulled me aside to ask if he could pray for me. What I told him still surprises me: "I don't need prayer. I just need help."

In my quest to save the Balkans, I had become a self-appointed messiah. The challenges, bureaucracy, and barriers were all whispers from God even though I didn't recognize them at the time. Through my frustration he was effectively saying, *There is a better way to do this.*

People tend to lean toward one of two extremes. Some, like me, are tempted to work from their own strength as if everything depends on them. That always leads to exhaustion, tension, and frustration. Others defer to divine intervention for a solution. They believe the world is *not* ours to save.[29] Only God can, and he should.

Unfortunately, our reluctance to build "God's kingdom by our own efforts," said N. T. Wright, "can actually be a way of hiding from responsibility, of keeping one's head down when the boss is looking for volunteers."[30] As a result, people may be inclined to excuse themselves from engagement and associated hard work. They may justify it with theology, standing on the sidelines while hoping God will miraculously do something. Faith gets a bad name as a result.

There is a middle way, however, that involves both hard work *and* sustained surrender to God so that his strength, his power, works in and through us. This principle acknowledges one of the great mysteries, and privileges, of our life with God: we are invited to be the hands and feet of Christ for others, offering the resurrection power of God to bring his healing, his solutions, his salvation to a broken world. As we've seen, Jesus and Paul were startlingly clear on this principle, yet it's rarely talked about. Why? Because we are afraid to elevate the expectations of those we lead, and even ourselves, only to disappoint later. Yet a disciple is "anyone whose ultimate goal is to live as Jesus would live if he were in their place."[31]

What would Jesus do in our place?

The great mystery of following Jesus is that he lives his life through us. Paul said, "I can do everything through him who gives me strength."[32] God didn't say it would be easy, but he promised help along the way:

Fear not, for I have redeemed you;
　　I have summoned you by name; you are mine.
When you pass through the waters,
　　I will be with you;
and when you pass through the rivers,
　　they will not sweep over you.
When you walk through the fire,
　　you will not be burned;
　　the flames will not set you ablaze.[33]

the poor too

If *all* people are called, what about the people affected most: the poor and oppressed?

The earthquake in Haiti killed an estimated three hundred thousand people. When I arrived, the airport was dark and eerily silent. But not the city. Guttural cries of grief swelled in waves from streets, homes, and make-shift hospitals. Bodies were strewn everywhere—children lay lifeless in the rubble, their hands clasped to their dead mothers or fathers. One little girl, covered in concrete dust, clutched her rag doll. The smell of death was inescapable.

I had never experienced anything like this. My heart still hurts when I think about it today. But it wasn't the suffering and the sorrow and grief that changed me most.

During the earthquake one mother ran back into her home to throw her body across her infant son, sacrificing her life so he could live. In the early hours following the disaster, Haitians performed their own search and rescue, pulling not only their loved ones from the rubble but complete strangers as well. Clergy provided shelter, food, and water in their churches. Local doctors, some without proper equipment or even anesthesia, saved thousands. Children sang songs in French and Creole well into the night to calm their trepidation. And people shared one another's grief.

In the middle of one of the greatest human tragedies, I discovered unlikely heroes changing their world. Their heroism still moves me to tears.

If victims can be heroes during an earthquake of such magnitude, what about the rest of the world where the suffering is no less real but less acute?

Nicholas, a good friend from our days living in Rwanda, fled his country's genocide in 1994 with his wife and newborn child. While in exile he studied, among other things, agronomy, earning a PhD from the University of Edinburgh. When he returned to Rwanda, he began a conversation with a group of rural women, most of whom had lost their families, about forming a community to distill essential oils. They created an association called Twizamura ("Let's grow together") to grow geranium, lemon grass, and eucalyptus. Following their harvest and the process of distilling geranium into oil, they export it internationally for use in perfume and aromatherapy.

Agnes also fled Rwanda when her husband was killed in the genocide. She was "lonely and without hope" when she returned to Rwanda with only her daughter—until she met the women of Twizamura. The women gave Agnes a few iron sheets to build a simple house. They asked her to join their association. Today her geranium leaf is distilled into oil and sold to South Africa and Europe, and she is serving her sisters as the president of Twizamura.

Inspired by Nicholas, Agnes and the women of Twizamura envisioned together, created a solution together, and implemented it together. They are changing their world.

If we zoom out and consider whole movements of change, we don't have to look too far. The microfinance movement, for example, is fueled by the ingenuity and responsibility of millions of entrepreneurs the world had previously written off as too poor to create and sustain businesses, pay loans, or save. The same is true in the health field. I've met hundreds of mothers who represent thousands more who are changing the health of their children using their own resources.

But isn't it fair to say there are some people who are too poor or unwilling or incapable of changing the world? Yes, there are. But they are far fewer than we think.

When we radically shift our ideas about those who suffer, seeing them not only as victims but as people with enormous resilience, creativity, unwavering hope, and indeed calling, we begin to think about poverty and injustice in very different ways. When those who need help become part of the solution, everything changes, from ownership of the problem to sustainability of the solution to the dignity of the people who rise up to overcome.

Understanding who we are in Christ will sober and stun us. We discover a God who radically invites everyone to follow him. Whether we choose to follow or not doesn't change his offer: *he wants to redeem the world through us*—his power, his plan, his grace *through* our hands, our feet, our minds, and our lives, *all* lives, the poor and oppressed included. In the words of Gary Haugen from International Justice Mission, "God has no plan B. We are it."[34]

There's more to you than you know.

FOUR

awakening your life

This first glance of a soul which does not
yet know itself is like dawn in the heavens;
it is the awakening of something radiant
and unknown.

—VICTOR HUGO, *LES MISÉRABLES*

Maybe you are convinced that changing the world is not just for a few but for everyone. But you might be less sure how to discover such a calling for yourself.

Years ago in the Canary Islands off the coast of North Africa, an otherwise ordinary British woman asked if she could pray for me. I politely obliged. I don't remember her name and barely remember her face, but I've never forgotten her prayer. She prayed from Isaiah 42, telling me its words would be important for my life. The themes were astonishing, especially for someone who, at the time, defined himself as *just* a business consultant from Wisconsin. Isaiah speaks of justice for the nations, opening eyes that are blind, freeing captives from prison, and releasing those who sit in darkness. As the evening sun splashed a red swath across the island city of Santa Cruz, she concluded her prayer with the following words:

See, the former things have taken place,
and new things I declare;
before they spring into being
I announce them to you.[1]

A cryptic prayer by an unlikely British woman quoting an ancient prophet turned my world upside down. In the days and weeks that followed, I began to envision a new future. My prayer life began to soar. We extended our stay in Africa as a result.

But then I began to experience anything *but* these words from Isaiah. I expected to fulfill a vision, but God led me into a season of intense struggle instead.

My season, however, turned out to be a gift in disguise. At the time I didn't know it was necessary for the breakthrough just around the corner. I spent the next handful of years in West Africa, working with people who literally gave sight to the blind through glaucoma and cataract surgeries. And through my role at World Relief today, I serve a staff of several thousand who release tens of thousands from the evils of poverty, injustice, and oppression.

What I thought would be a perfunctory prayer became a blueprint for my life. I would never have believed a few paragraphs from Isaiah, spoken over me on a remote island across the world, would be fulfilled over years, indeed a lifetime.

an unexpected adventure

My experience wasn't unique. The more I followed the lives of others, the more I began to see a pattern. Like me, people I encountered seemed to begin their journey with a revelation of sorts, a visionary idea, a burst of intuition or inspiration, a moment when heaven broke through. But then something generally went wrong. Trials suddenly emerged—sometimes hellacious ones—putting their moments of clarity to the test. Deep disappointment set in, and as a result many gave up. Some even questioned God.

But for those who didn't, suffering served to forge a calling. Their vision became real, their character deep, and their courage strong.

Years ago a friend of mine set out to change the world by joining a ministry in South Africa. He quickly assumed a leadership role. But his calling didn't emerge as he had expected. Instead, he found himself in a disappointing relationship and a conflict with another leader. He was completely disheartened.

But instead of giving up, he prayed and fasted for twenty-one days. He returned home to England to undertake studies while working in his local parish. A few years later, at the height of the turmoil in Afghanistan, he launched a nonprofit focused on the plight of Afghan women and children. He eventually moved to Afghanistan, leading his organization from Kabul. Today we celebrate his impact even as he continues to expand his vision.

God needed to change my friend before he could bring change through him.

As compelling as his story is, it is only one of many.

When I look back, I can separate the people I know into two groups. Many put aside their visions and plans and settled for tempered lives—not necessarily bad ones, but tempered. Some chalked up those days of inspiration and vision to youthful pipe dreams not anchored in reality. Worse, others dismissed their experiences outright, blaming faith or even God for promises not kept. Most who chose this road seemed happy on the outside but empty on the inside, resorting to "lives of quiet desperation," as Thoreau said.[2]

But others pushed through their challenges, never losing hope, never giving up their promise, their visions, their dreams. And somehow along the way, they experienced a breakthrough and emerged from their trials flourishing.

When I look to the Bible, I find the same pattern: first, a vision, sometimes a mountaintop experience, a glimpse of the future; then a descent into the valley, where the vision is often veiled and the terrain arduous; and then a breakthrough beyond the forest, to the beautiful city or dwelling, where the vision begins to flourish.

A glimpse followed by descent followed by a breakthrough. If you look, you will see this pattern everywhere.

David was anointed king when he was a mere shepherd boy. But he went back to his fields until he was called into service to Saul. He defeated Goliath, but then his leader tried to kill him. He was all but banished for years, on the run, under threat, until he was eventually installed as king of Israel.

Joseph had a dream but was sold by his brothers into slavery. He languished in prison until Pharaoh promoted him to second-in-command of Egypt, where his dream was finally fulfilled.

Gabriel visited Mary with news of great joy, but she experienced anything but joy until the birth of her son, whom shepherds, and later kings, worshiped.

Paul was ambushed by God with blinding light but then disappeared until Barnabas found him and helped establish him as an apostle.

Even Jesus lived the pattern. At age twelve he glimpsed his future and began teaching in the temple. But his promise didn't commence for another eighteen years. He may have wondered why it took so long, maybe even experiencing disappointment along the way.

We find the same pattern in Mandela, Lincoln, Mother Teresa, and so many others.

Joseph Campbell called this pattern the archetypal "monomyth," the hero's journey from status quo to the unknown, where she or he overcomes trials with supernatural help, changes the world, and, in so doing, returns home permanently changed.[3] We see and experience this monomyth in literature, film, history, and daily life. A surprising character reinvents herself through a journey into the unknown. An insecure person understands who he is only after he takes a risk, his identity forged in crisis.

But is the hero's journey reserved for only some? What if this myth, this blueprint, is a divine pattern for all of us—an archetypal awakening, a pathway God himself chose to live out as a carpenter from Nazareth? If, in fact, there is a divine pattern here, how do we lean into it? Where do we begin?

glimpse

My experience in the Canary Islands actually had its genesis much earlier. One Saturday morning while cycling on a trail outside of Madison, Wisconsin, I was overcome with the question of whether I had really given my whole life to God. Several years before, in a flood of tears, I had surrendered to him, and my life had radically changed as a result. I had become less self-centered and certainly more focused on living a more virtuous life than the prodigal one I had lived before. But if I had given God my worst then, was I giving God my best now?

I stopped near a wooden bridge along the tree-lined trail. I felt compelled to confess my love for God right there on that bridge as a few people jogged by. I wanted to do something significant, covenantal. I felt foolish; my heart began to pound. But somehow I cast aside my embarrassment and cried out, "God, I love you!" Then I prayed, *God, don't ever elevate me above my ability to handle it. You are more important than my success. I am willing to do anything, go anywhere, for you. My life is yours.*

I am convinced my adventure into changing the world began with a seemingly foolish moment on a wooded trail in rural Wisconsin.

God often gives us a glimpse of our calling but not the full picture. Sometimes he waits for us to make the first move. Experiences usually come in stages, and they are more commonplace than we think. Sometimes they are so commonplace it's hard to know if God is even speaking. I am often unsure whether God is speaking to me at all, so I write things down—scriptures, inspired thoughts, even the quiet, inner voice. I worry less about immediately trying to determine if something is from God and, instead, seek to confirm it over time.

You may expect your calling to come suddenly, mysteriously, or even shockingly. But how many people do you know with stories like that? We tend to forget the people in the Bible who lacked a mountaintop experience—Luke, Lydia, and Barnabas to name a few. Yet they were just as called.

The pursuit of calling is hard work, requiring imagination, faith, and grit. One of my African friends grew up herding cows but had an insatiable hunger to go to school. So he sneaked into the local school to learn. He was whipped for attending, however, because he wasn't meant to be at school. But he kept going until his teachers noticed he was smart and willing. Today, with a master's degree, he influences thousands, especially church leaders, by showing them how to serve their communities. He's an inspiration to many because he imagined, believed, and didn't give up.

Calling begins with listening during the common places of life, the ordinary events, even the daily drudgery. "Every common bush is afire with God," said Elizabeth Barrett Browning.[4] Paradoxically, while the journey of calling may be arduous, there are times when God seems to speak incessantly. Frederick Buechner said:

> There is no event so commonplace that God is not present in it,
> always hiddenly, always leaving you room to recognize him or not
> recognize him. . . . Listen to your life. See it for the fathomless mystery
> that it is. In the boredom and the pain of it no less than in the

excitement and the gladness: touch, taste, smell your way to the holy and hidden heart of it because in the last analysis all moments are key moments, and life itself is grace.[5]

Over months, and sometimes years, of pursuing calling, themes emerge. Coincidental words, thoughts, experiences suddenly lose their arbitrary nature. Scriptures, words, images, and experiences appearing first without pattern or symmetry eventually weave together to take form. An uncommon beauty appears. Wisdom rises. The scribbles in your journal start to make sense.

God begins to awaken your life.

Sometimes discovering your calling is easier with friends. Several years ago while attending Saint Brendan's in Washington, DC, we encountered a discernment process that involved a group of friends. At the time Belinda and I were faced with a significant decision related to our calling that would affect not only us but also our kids. The stakes were high. We needed a glimpse from God, but we were at a loss. So a group of friends led us though a listening process to better understand God's perspective on the decision we faced and to clarify our calling. We've rarely experienced anything so helpful, practical, and kind. Friends helped us steward our lives. We were humbled and honored.

Some might describe vision and calling—what I am referring to here as *glimpse*—as two different things. In the Bible, vision is about the future, whether through revelation, a prophecy, or a dream. Bill Hybels calls vision "a picture of the future that creates passion in people."[6] Calling, on the other hand, as we learned, is more nuanced. It includes elements of both identity and vocation, involving specific tasks and responsibilities for the future.

But calling and vision often come together, and for all the subjectivity surrounding their discovery, there are practical ways to pursue and understand both. But the goal is always the same: to steward your life well in light of God's purposes. The journey is important, not the pace or the manner in which you tread. God will lead you carefully, even if not always comfortably.

I believe God longs to speak to everyone in surprising ways through everyday life. Calling begins right *where you are, as you are,* "the place where your deep gladness and the world's deep hunger meet,"[7] whether with a group of friends or alone with God.

descent

After the glimpse comes the descent.

In my late twenties I served several hundred staff in a leadership position in West Africa. Most people would say we were on the front lines. The blind saw, the lame walked, death was overcome, and not solely through medicine and surgeries; we saw miracles too. The words from Isaiah 42 became part of my daily life. It was challenging, sometimes overwhelming, but always thrilling.

We were convinced we had found our lifelong calling.

But then everything went wrong. Belinda and I exhausted ourselves; we justified it with the needs all around us. There was a war one country away. We evacuated people. There were staff members with life issues. We counseled them well into the night. There were opportunities that seemed impossible to pass up. We jetted around the continent and into Europe to seize the day.

Then I found myself in a conflict with another leader. I had little personal reserve to navigate it well. We fell out of friendship, and after several months I resigned my leadership role. I would have been fired had I not. My world collapsed and, with it, our dreams.

Three months later, following a stint of counseling for clinical burnout, we transferred to our organization's home office to work alongside several trusted mentors. We had just learned we were unable to have children. Our personal funding—we were self-supported in those days—had all but stalled. I was in such poor health physically, emotionally, and mentally that I literally struggled to string more than a few thoughts together. Now, in a half-time administrative role—the intent was an honorable way to convalesce—I was printing nametags for the leadership council to which I previously belonged. I was no longer part of the team. I felt looked down upon, as one who had lost it somehow.

I was humiliated.

In the words of Dante, "I woke up in the middle of my life and found myself in a dark wood."[8] I had become addicted to the limelight, to leadership rather than the goal, to ministry rather than God. My relationship with Belinda was beginning to chafe. My mind, heart, and soul were simultaneously scattered and tethered.

My dark night lasted several years, an experience that became, in the words of Lewis, "the most brutal of teachers."[9]

But I wouldn't trade those lessons for the world. So much of who I am today I learned in that cauldron. God had led me kicking and screaming into a descent. What I thought was cruel turned out to be a rescue operation. In the valley I could no longer see the vision or the call. I was forced to focus on my character instead. In the descent God helped me reset and align my core motivations and ambitions with his. In the surrender I exchanged superficial elements of leadership for a version that was more enduring, less selfish. My life turned upside down and inside out, but I came out the other side stronger.

Thank God for his mercy, which, at the time, felt harsh. Now I see it differently.

breakthrough

When we did our stint of counseling in southern France, spring hadn't hatched yet. The grapevines were just pruned—so severely cut back that, for a viticulture novice like me, it seemed they were dead. I was reminded of the text in the Gospels:

Every branch in Me that does not bear fruit He takes away, and every branch that bears fruit He prunes, that it may bear more fruit.[10]

In the foothills of Mont Blanc, where all I could do spiritually was pray the Lord's Prayer once a day, I learned that dying and pruning feel the same. Both involve cutting away the old to make way for new life. One is permanent, when viewed from this side of life, while the other is temporary. But they feel the same. I felt alone, and thus I clung to my Savior all the more. At times I felt the pain associated with utter failure. But the purpose of pruning is to increase fruit, not kill it. God helped me re-anchor my life, my identity, in him rather than in what I do, an invaluable truth. In that season I learned that the tallest trees have the deepest roots. And roots spread wide during times of storms and wind; they go deeper during times of drought.

You may recognize this as nothing more than mere Christianity: God gives; he takes away—all for our good.

You may have more experience with valleys and descents and dark nights than I do. Perhaps your childhood was one long, dark night. Or your own child is suffering, whether self-inflicted or not. Or you've lived a life of quiet desperation for so long that you've lost your way. My experience taught me many things but one essential principle: God leads us into descent because he has something greater in mind. His motive is love, and his objective is good.

Trust him.

And don't give up before your breakthrough:

> Every great work, every great accomplishment, has been brought into manifestation through holding to the vision, and often just before the big achievement, comes apparent failure and discouragement.[11]

And when you fail, remember the company of saints. Peter failed miserably; he denied Christ three times after promising to join him in his death. Paul failed his Lord until his encounter with him on a Damascus road and later fell out with the man who vouched for him among the apostles.

If there is grace for them, there is grace for you and me. Paul said, "I press on to take hold of that for which Christ Jesus took hold of me."[12] Some days I have to repeat this to pick myself up off the mat. Grace may seem thin at first, but it's thick and tangible in the end. Hang on to it; don't let it go. Its promise to console and liberate will come, even if it tarries.

It is during the descending moments of our lives that we have the opportunity to change the most. Suffering is a good teacher. But we are not alone.

> Paul does not say "that we might *know about* the righteousness of God," nor "that we might *believe in* the righteousness of God," nor even "that we might *receive* the righteousness of God." Instead, [we are] to *become* the righteousness of God: where [we together] embody . . . the world-reconciling love of Jesus Christ.[13]

The lesson in the hero's journey, the dark night of the soul, and the season of suffering is clear: trials, confusion, disappointment, and even disillusionment are essential for our impending breakthrough. Descents are required to prepare us for greater vision because calling rests first upon our character.

Without it, we cave, just as I did. We have the greatest potential to convert our *doing* into a process of *becoming* during our descents. Self-discovery during difficult seasons is fruitful and often surprising.

Authority to change the world flows first from who we are, not what we say or do. What we learn through disappointment, discouragement, or downright disillusionment makes us who we are and gives us the authority to influence change, sometimes well beyond our dreams. There's purpose, even virtue, in our suffering if we are brave enough to accept its wisdom.

Jesus said, "You did not choose me, but I chose you and appointed you so that you might go and bear fruit—fruit that will last."[14] The God of the universe wants you to flourish. Believing this to be true is the hardest part, especially during the dark night of your descent.

Jesus restored Peter on the beach. Mary gave birth to a Savior. Mandela shed his prison for a palace. My friend launched his dream in Afghanistan.

Heroes brave enough to pursue their journey experience breakthroughs. Your breakthrough is just around the corner. Don't give up.

a say in the matter

You may still be wondering why it's so difficult to discover your calling.

When I was young, I dreamed of becoming a rock star. I learned to play the drum kit when I was six, and by age nine I was playing in a band most weekends to crowds of hundreds. Ours was a Wisconsin family wedding band with a repertoire that spanned the musical genres from "The Beer Barrel Polka" to "Twist and Shout." My father was the bandleader or better, the entrepreneur extraordinaire who reinvented a rural Wisconsin family into a modern-day Von Trapp family. My mother carried the vocals, her life story remarkably similar to Maria's in *The Sound of Music*. The high-water mark of most evenings was a rendition of "The Chicken Dance" where the crowd flapped their arms and stomped their feet to an ever-increasing tempo set by the boy drummer.

But it wasn't until I discovered jazz that I began to really understand the power of music. Jazz is set apart in the musical spectrum in this way: when a group of jazz musicians begin a song, they don't have it all worked out. They improvise along the way, playing off the others' gifts, setting up each other for comps and riffs and rhythms and melodies. In Ken Burns's classic documentary about the history of jazz, Wynton Marsalis put it this way:

> Jazz music is an art that gives us a penniless way to understand ourselves. The real power of jazz, the real innovation of jazz is that a group of people can come together and create art, improvised art, and can negotiate their agendas together. . . . We can have a dialogue. We can have a conversation. We can speak to each other in the language of music.[15]

Awakening your life is like finding your way through a jazz solo. God could certainly tell us all at once, in simple, more direct ways. But instead he invites us to craft it with him, in relationship, through the messiness, in the midst of all our questions. The basic structure is there—a chord progression, the rhythms, even the key—but the exact tune must be discovered with God. He gives us a voice, a say in the matter, a certain freedom for self-expression in crafting our lives.

learning how

You likely know that personal change is generally accomplished not with broad, sweeping leaps but with daily steps. Calling is discovered over a lifetime, especially as we act on our calling along the way. And whether we are on the mountaintop or in the valley, virtue is learned over months and sometimes years, not days or all at once.

Scholars say self-discipline predicts performance more than intelligence, and willpower is the paramount factor for individual success. But behind willpower and self-discipline is something simpler: *habits.* Charles Duhigg, author of *The Power of Habit,* said habits create "neurological cravings," subconscious desires in our brains to fulfill something we've learned.[16] In sum, what we do every day has the potential to determine what we can accomplish over the span of our lives.

In the sixth century a monk by the name of Benedict created a set of precepts, which he called a Rule, to guide his community in France. The idea of a rule comes from the Greek word for "trellis,"[17] a tool that enables a vine to grow above the ground so it can produce more fruit. Benedict's Rule was a kind of trellis for people, a book of habits for living a more fruitful life, both religious and practical. Over the centuries many have looked to Benedict's Rule to guide their communities. Today people create their own Rule of Life[18] to concentrate their daily habits on things they care about most, whether God, family, or important pursuits.

A Rule of Life typically centers on the personal and contemplative, a daily rhythm to nurture important relationships with a special focus on God. But a Rule of Life can also prioritize the needs of others. Investing in certain habits can change us so we can influence others. And more often than not, it works in the reverse too. Habits allow us to meaningfully engage the world so we can personally change.

If you are willing to work hard—and especially if you are going through a dark night or coming through a season of disappointment—consider creating your own rule, a personal set of habits to help you discover your calling and live differently.

Begin by simply listening to your life. As you listen to and wrestle with the call awakening in you, capture its message. Consider both your ordinary and extraordinary encounters, and invest in their counsel.

For me, pursuing calling is not natural. Unfortunately I tend to *do* first and listen later. Maybe you are like me. But God always seems to ambush me with reminders of who I am—the message in an untimely failure, the counsel in the words of a friend, or the wisdom in a poignant scripture. I have come to believe that our identity *in God* is absolutely foundational to doing anything *for God*. When the former weakens, the latter falls. For me, it takes intentional discipline and habits to help me do the hard work of listening.

As you listen to your life, distill what God is saying to you. In your journal jot down words that are supremely important to you. Reflect on the words in your lament. Begin to join these phrases and words into a calling statement. What you develop could very well guide you for years to come, even if it evolves along the way. Mine has been supremely helpful to me. It's simple because it's meant to accompany a text from Isaiah.

I belong to God, who loves me and has chosen me. I am called to inspire people to take radical steps toward bringing justice to a suffering world.

As you press into your calling, continue to silence that sinister voice that might whisper, *You are not called.* Let's debunk the myth that surrounds calling: your calling and mine are fixed and firm and etched in the heavens and waiting to be awakened.

confessing and committing

Two other habits have been especially important to Belinda and me as we've sought to awaken and live out our call: *confessing* and *committing.*

The act of confessing typically implies something needs correcting. But it means so much more. Its root word simply means "to agree, admit, or acknowledge," creating the potential to "place one in harmony with others."[19] In Hebrew the word for "confess" implies a conviction of the heart or a change of conviction and therefore is associated with acknowledging wrongdoing, whether by commission or omission.

When it comes to suffering and injustice, confession means to acknowledge those who suffer, to see them, to listen to them. When we validate their stories, we validate them; we give them dignity. Confession also acknowledges our own pain and sometimes our failures too, including our failure to care. When we confess, we begin to care. And caring changes us.

When it comes to the entrenched issues surrounding injustice, commitment matters too. I find myself needing to recommit regularly to God at key moments in my life. Sometimes it's as simple as committing to a project or something physical—a marathon or 5K—as an act of solidarity, or perseverance for something greater.

Without genuine commitment we risk setting out on a journey we cannot finish. What specific habits might inform and deepen your commitment? Maybe it's understanding the stories of those trapped in an area of injustice. You might find a way to meet with someone who's suffered—for example, a refugee family from Iraq, Sudan, or Burma who is living near you.

Over time habits like these can increase your capacity in surprising ways. You might begin to learn a language so you can relate to immigrants in your hometown as well as to their families across the world. Or you might take a course in microfinance, ethics, or community health from your local college or online. You may want to increase your understanding of justice, for example, by taking a course in social ethics. Volunteering to teach English to Bhutanese refugees will increase their capacity and your empathy. Doing self-study on ethnic reconciliation would increase your capacity to engage more meaningfully in a multiethnic church or community setting.

As you create your personal rule, aim for less rather than more. Try living out your habits with a friend or your small group. You may need to tweak them along the way. Find ways to test your growth. Are you increasingly willing to offer yourself to God? to take risks with others? Are you more honest with yourself? Are you experiencing an increase in your capacity, especially in the specific areas in which you want to grow?

Your personal rule may very well surprise you. What has shaped communities and people for centuries still works today.

As G. K. Chesterton said, all people matter: "You matter. I matter. It's the hardest thing in theology to believe."[20] Calling is worthy of our honest pursuit, even if arduous at times, because we know virtue is learned more through seasons of disappointment than seasons of daffodils. We may, at times, have to muster our faith to believe, clear our vision to see, and unplug our ears to hear. When we do, all that's left is the courage to live it out and the hard work to awaken what is waiting inside us. If the world contains the latent capacity to sing a new song, then let it start with us.

Part II

Reframing the Problem

FIVE

six impossibilities
before breakfast

Some things have to be believed to
be seen.
—MADELEINE L'ENGLE

I have no problem with miracles. I am
living around them. I am one.
—BONO

In a scene from Lewis Carroll's *Alice in Wonderland,* the White Queen
lectures Alice on believing the impossible:

"I can't believe that!" said Alice.

"Can't you?" the Queen said in a pitying tone. "Try again: draw a
long breath, and shut your eyes."

Alice laughed. "There's no use trying," she said: "one can't believe
impossible things."

"I daresay you haven't had much practice," said the Queen.

"When I was your age, I always did it for half-an-hour a day. Why, sometimes I've believed as many as six impossible things before breakfast."[1]

Through the White Queen, Carroll eloquently says that unless we believe, we'll never see. Faith leads to vision, not the other way around, and vision is indispensable to change.

But we often shrink from big ideas.

Recovering our call is a chief cornerstone for creating change. But reframing the problem is an equally essential one. And reframing requires us to think big.

Too often we tackle age-old problems of poverty or injustice by retreading ideas that have failed. Sometimes we give up because we are convinced the problems are impossible to overcome. Or worse, we don't even try because certain versions of faith tell us not to get involved.

But what if the impossibilities that leave you and me hopeless or paralyzed secretly burst with truth and promise? What if we were to believe just a few impossible things?

In the words of the White Queen, we need more practice.

Certain themes concerning faith, poverty, and injustice often leave people cynical or even hopeless. You may have heard phrases like "It will never change" or "Faith does more harm than good" or "We don't need God to do good." What if we were to take the White Queen's advice and reframe these perennial impossibilities into possibilities, setting aside for a moment our skepticism so we can rethink these conundrums?

If we believe that the poor *can*, in fact, change the world and that God invites *all* of us—whether poor, rich, or in-between—to join him in saving the world, then we are ready to look at the problem of suffering through a different lens, both theologically and practically. The implications of doing so are significant.

Let's begin by considering two "impossibilities" about poverty and faith: *faith does more good than harm* and *we cannot do good without God.*

faith does more good than harm

Atheists say that faith damages thought, culture, and science; that it holds people in ignorance and fear; that it uses old texts to condone and entrench faulty thinking; that it serves the needs of those in power and privilege more than those in want. In essence, that faith does more harm than good.

A journalist once asked me if doing justice in the name of Jesus is a good thing considering the injustice caused by religion throughout history. "What if we were to count the dead bodies stacked up in the name of religion?" he asked.[2] He referenced the Crusades, slavery, and colonialism and pointed out how the global church was late in responding to the HIV/AIDS epidemic.

"Could we also count the missing bodies?" I asked. What if Africa's suffering had never "arrested" William Wilberforce's heart?[3] What if a young girl from Albania had never listened to a call to serve the dying in India? What if Desmond Tutu had never laid his body across a white man about to be stoned by an angry mob? What if Jesus Christ had never taken upon himself the violence of the world so that one day all violence would cease?

"How many bodies would be stacked up then?" I asked.

A decade after the genocide in Rwanda, in which eight hundred thousand to a million people were slaughtered in one hundred days, I knelt with my sons, Joshua and Caleb, then ages five and three, at the site of a mass grave near the capital city of Kigali. We placed flowers for the children who had lost their lives.

"How could people who love God do this to one another?" Joshua asked. I paused, having asked myself the same question many times. "Even in the horror," I said, "there were people who demonstrated astonishing faith." I told them about Iphigenia Mukantabana, who regularly shares a meal with Jean-Bosco and his wife. Eleven years before, Iphigenia's husband and five children were clubbed to death during the genocide. Jean-Bosco was one of the murderers. After his release from prison, Jean-Bosco asked Iphigenia for forgiveness. For years she refused, saying she was unable to speak to him. But over time her heart softened. She realized reconciliation would not happen unless she opened her heart and accepted his pleas.[4] Today Iphigenia and Jean-Bosco drink tea together, setting a precedent of friendship, instead of revenge, for the generations that follow.

In one corner of the world, the body count stopped.

Whether faith does more harm than good depends upon what we mean by *faith*. If by *faith* we mean a set of creedal beliefs without a genuine demonstration of those beliefs, then I agree with my atheist friends. But if we judge faith by its deeds, we get an entirely different result. Iphigenia is living proof.

Deeds tell the real story of faith. They differentiate true religion from false, and they say a whole lot more about the quality of our faith than words do. While people are never redeemed through their works—only God redeems—faith that does not produce good works is dead. Of course, this doesn't mean people will never fail. Genuine followers of Jesus still sin. But those who turn from their ways actually "bear fruit in keeping with repentance."[5] One proof of genuine faith is how we serve the least of these. We know from the oft-read passage in the gospel of Matthew that when we serve the most vulnerable, we are effectively serving Jesus:

"Lord, when did we see you hungry and feed you, or thirsty and give you something to drink? When did we see you a stranger and invite you in, or needing clothes and clothe you? When did we see you sick or in prison and go to visit you?"

The King will reply, "Truly I tell you, whatever you did for one of the least of these . . . you did for me."[6]

why nature trumps name

Some followers of Jesus talk more often about the kingdom of God than about changing the world. And for good reason. Jesus used this phrase frequently; many say it was his life theme. But kings and kingdoms were common in his day, while they are foreign to us, archaic actually, even fearful. Dallas Willard has defined the kingdom of God as simply "the range of [God's] effective will,"[7] based on Jesus's own definition in his prayer: "Your kingdom come, your will be done on earth as it is in heaven."[8] When we do good, we establish the will of God on earth. We fulfill the prayer of Jesus.

To pray or act in God's name, then, means we are implementing his will. In Jesus's day a name represented a person's nature and character because it provided the general parameters for his or her will. By invoking a name, you were invoking the nature and character of that person. So when you entered a covenant, you were committing not only your name, reputation, wealth, and strength but your character as well.

In Jewish culture, wisdom is proved by how one lives. Calling ourselves by a name and then acting in ways contrary to the nature of that name is deeply problematic. A person who openly confesses Jesus but intentionally acts in ways contrary to the nature of Jesus desecrates his nature and therefore his name too. There are obvious examples from history. The union of cross and sword in the Crusades is one. The conquest of the Americas through genocide is another. When we kill, steal, and destroy in the name of Christ, we undermine the very name and reputation we seek to honor.

In recounting the Sermon on the Mount, Matthew and Luke distilled the central message of Jesus into a collection of sayings that have inspired, threatened, and confounded the world ever since. Take, for example, his thoughts on conflict: "You have heard that it was said, 'Love your neighbor and hate your enemy.' But I tell you, love your enemies and pray for those who persecute you."[9] What if history had taken these words more seriously during the Crusades? Or what if long ago we had applied these words to the other tribe, color, class, or gender?

An organization, church, initiative, or program is only truly Christian insofar as it functions according to the nature of Jesus. If any community— whether church, government, or business—functions in ways opposed to the nature of Jesus, it falls on the side of evil, whether it knows it or not. In effect, it opposes the will of God. It doesn't matter what we call it. It doesn't matter who does it. Unfortunately, well-intended people, followers of Jesus included, oppose God all the time; they just don't realize it. Anything contrary to the will of God is actually taking life away rather than creating it. Followers talk about "building" and "bringing" the kingdom of God. But we may be destroying it instead. The Bible is clear enough: faith without good deeds is dead.[10]

Faith has been blamed for all sorts of evil through the centuries. But actions taken in the *name* of God but not in his *nature* are not just. Many times they are evil. The nature of our actions, not the name we claim, is the differentiator.

we cannot do good without God

You may have seen, or even experienced, the harm created by bad religion or by evil masquerading as religion. But genuine faith, *true religion,* brings healing to a broken world. Consider the great litany of saints, from Mother Teresa to Francis of Assisi to William Cary to the countless, nameless heroes who change the world every day in the name of God. We are indebted to them.

But do we really need God in order to do good? We all know people who don't proclaim to follow Jesus yet do good works, including passionately caring about justice. How do we explain this?

divine rights

When it comes to saving the world, contemporary thinkers often look to human rights as a basis for doing good. While human rights theory has been around since the Renaissance, it gained prominence following World War II, especially in view of the Holocaust. Philosophers looked to the theories of John Locke and others, their thinking inspired by Judeo-Christian thought, culminating with Thomas Jefferson's Declaration of Independence, a document that has been inspiring change since 1776: "We hold these truths to be self-evident, that all men are created equal, that they are endowed by their Creator with certain unalienable Rights . . ."[11]

But during the Enlightenment, God disappeared from human rights theory. Article 1 of the United Nations Universal Declaration of Human Rights reads: "All human beings are born free and equal in dignity and rights. They are endowed with reason and conscience and should act towards one another in a spirit of brotherhood."[12]

While some might argue the use of "endowed" assumes a Creator, the missing reference to God was intentional. The United Nations sought to create a framework comparable to the Judeo-Christian ethical system yet without a theological basis. It was based instead strictly on natural law.

But human rights without God leads to more problems than solutions. If one assumes the role of an atheist, then one usually reaches for evolution to describe the world around him. Evolution, in its strictest, moral sense, removes all values, including the idea of any "good." We are, in essence, only the product of chemical reactions brought about by chance over time. If that is true, we have no basis for good and evil, morality, human rights, or even human dignity. One would be hard pressed to seek justice when it doesn't ultimately matter.

If we include the divine as the basis for human rights, then we must presuppose that such a divine being is fundamentally good. If the divine being is capricious or arbitrary, the basis for human rights theory breaks down. We are left without a foundation.

The Judeo-Christian ethic, upon which human rights theory is implicitly based, presents God as fundamentally good, loving, and just. Without this foundation any claim for ultimate good slips away. Evil, the violation of that ultimate good, becomes inexplicable. Instead, the Judeo-Christian ethic shows the world that the evil we experience in this life is not the intention or ultimate will of God. In fact, God even redeems evil waged against us to bring about ultimate goodness.[13]

Human rights are defensible only when they are anchored in the *Imago Dei*—the idea that God created human beings in his image and, in doing so, conferred incomprehensible value on all human life. He loves all people no matter who we are or what we've done. And those who pursue the dignity of every human being are motivated intrinsically by a profound idea: God commands us to love one another just as he loves us.

Some of the earliest acts of compassion are linked directly to the idea of *Imago Dei*. In the fourth century Basil of Caesarea, known for his care of the poor and destitute, asked, "What if we build a place of love and care of lepers?" His brother, Gregory of Nyssa, said, "Lepers have been made in the image of God. . . . Let us minister to Christ's needs. Let us give Christ nourishment. Let us clothe Christ. . . . Let us show Christ honor." With these words, the first hospital was born.[14]

Such acts of compassion have continued throughout history. Several years ago the Horn of Africa experienced one of its worst droughts in this century, leaving nearly 40 percent of children in parts of northwest Kenya severely malnourished.[15] Across the country, in the capital city of Nairobi, Pastor Simon of Parklands Baptist Church rallied his congregation to reach out to the nomadic people called the Turkana in northwest Kenya, whom most Kenyans considered unworthy to acknowledge, let alone help. Simon and Parklands Church organized emergency food relief, water, a nutrition intervention, and an agriculture program by inviting others—Wheaton Bible Church near Chicago, Grace Chapel in Boston, and World Relief—to join their cause. Today the Turkana are growing watermelons where there once was famine, and they have a vision to take what they've learned to other tribes facing the same devastation. All this began when a group of Kenyans chose to see the Turkana people as image bearers of God, indeed, their "neighbors." Just like Basil before him, Simon chose to serve the "least of these" because he believed the sick and disenfranchised to be worthy of certain fundamental rights.

grace in common

But what about the many people who genuinely do good without reference to faith, God, or any moral framework whatsoever, even human rights? Are they not, in essence, doing good *without* God?

In their minds *yes*. But what they don't realize is this: by nature of the *Imago Dei*, God gives them common grace, "which curbs the destructive power of sin, maintains in a measure the moral order of the universe . . . , distributes in varying degrees gifts and talents among men, promotes the development of science and art, and showers untold blessings upon" all people.[16]

Whether all those doing good realize it or not, they are doing good *with* God. Their good will not redeem their souls—only God can do that—but what they do is, in fact, genuine good, because it belongs to the God who gives common grace.

Still, we shouldn't depend upon common grace. *Good now* doesn't mean *good forever*. In the words of Russian literary hero Fyodor Dostoyevsky, "History has proven that good intentions towards mankind . . . without love toward God, can ultimately lead to coercion over mankind."[17]

In the end God and good are inextricably linked. We simply cannot do good without God.

reframing the problem of suffering

It shouldn't surprise us that Jesus and good are also linked. We've said the core message of Jesus is the "gospel of the kingdom," or simply the "gospel," which means, in essence, "good news." But what is good news today? Is it not that we can be free from pain, shame, wrongs, and suffering, temporally and eventually, once and for all? The gospel in its purest form puts suffering out of business, and it begins here and now.

People long for the gospel whether they are aware of it or not. But some would say that God saves a *person* from her wrongs, not the *world* from its wrongs—that the gospel is spiritual, not social. If the gospel is primarily, or even entirely, about saving us from our sins, then saving the world will exclusively mean evangelism, Bible translation, church building, training for ministry, and so on—*not* addressing physical needs, economic choices, or societal and political evils. But a person's standing with God doesn't necessarily fix how people stand with each other. In 1994 Rwanda was considered the most Christian country in the world. More than 90 percent of the population participated in weekly church services across the country.[18] Yet tens of thousands lifted machetes against their neighbors, friends, and even family members.

Mark Dever at Capitol Hill Baptist Church in Washington, DC, said we must understand the gospel on several levels. God focuses on the human heart and seeks a complete overhaul, but he also exchanges his zoom lens for a wide angle to look at the impact of changed lives in neighborhoods, communities, villages, and nations. His point? One lens without the other is incomplete. Heart change without a corresponding life change is deeply problematic, so much so that others may question the authenticity of our faith. Jesus called this hypocrisy, a strong critique from a carpenter turned teacher. He even said to those who showed no life change, "I never knew you; depart from Me."[19]

On the other hand, changing the world without genuine heart change often leads to control, greed, corruption, and eventually tyranny. History tells too many sordid stories to disagree.

If we shrink salvation down to an individualistic, abstract experience, people may be "saved but the social order is ignored."[20] We are left with a "crippled Christianity."[21] Prioritizing the spiritual above the material, the sacred over the secular, word above deed, and us over them gives God a black eye.

What if we refused to obsess about arguments that center on what *could* be God's will and instead wholeheartedly pursued what we *know* to be his will? Most agree that God is concerned with not only redeeming people but also, through them, bringing his will, his rule—as characterized by truth, peace, justice, and love—into *all* of life. He desires the restoration of all aspects—the economy, government, health, environment, education, business, and the arts—"right down to its basic structures."[22] God desires his will here "on earth as it is in heaven."[23] Ministry to the poor, naked, sick, hungry, and oppressed is not merely a means to an end but part and parcel of the very will of God.

Consider a young girl trapped in slavery. If somehow she surrendered her life to God and in that process, whether before or after, was offered physical freedom, restored health, an education, and a fulfilling career, what part would she say was the will of God? Only the spiritual?

Jesus engaged the whole spectrum of life—the social, economic, and spiritual. He redefined the ethics for each, and he prioritized the poor.[24] And Paul followed Jesus. He preached a "ministry of reconciliation," describing the implications of redemption not only for our souls but for all spheres of life, even the physical order.[25]

rediscovering justice

Viewing the problem of suffering and its solutions as part of the promise of the gospel may help us understand *why* but not necessarily *what* we should do or *how* we should do it. The biblical concept of justice is more helpful on these fronts. Anchored in the heart of God, justice has risen in clarity, scope, and stature in recent years to the extent that we are experiencing a recovery of its very meaning. Justice is being reclaimed, stolen back from social and political camps. What is emerging is something beautiful: an ancient but restored version of justice anchored deeply in the person and sacrificial love of Jesus and inseparable from the very essence of the gospel. As we recover its biblical meaning, we encounter a God who loves justice, demands justice, and executes it for the needy *through us*. And most important, justice helps us turn the problem of suffering upside down.

Let's explore how.

Two words are used for "justice" in the Old Testament. The first, *mishpat,* means "rendering judgment" or "giving people what they are due" and is sometimes referred to as "rectifying justice." The second word, *tsedeqa,* means "the right thing" or, especially, "right relationships" and is referred to as "primary justice." These words are often paired in Scripture as "justice and righteousness," and in some instances one means the other.[26] The book of

Isaiah even uses the word *justice* to mean "the sum total of what the Lord has adjudged to be right," or, in essence, the very will of God.[27]

Taken together, *mishpat* and *tsedeqa* present a relational definition of justice, an important dimension that has been overlooked for too long. They capture both the action of God, when referring to the relationship between God and his people, and also the conduct of his followers, when referring to social relationships. This should not surprise us, given the centrality of love in the Old and New Testaments. For example, "Love the LORD your God with all your heart and with all your soul and with all your strength,"[28] to which Jesus adds, "Love your neighbor as yourself."[29] This relational aspect is a pivotal dimension of justice, an insight recovered in recent years.[30]

In its fullness, justice is about right relationships—relationships that work. Injustice is about relationships that don't. Justice for the "Quartet of the Vulnerable"—the orphan, the widow, the immigrant, and the poor—is especially important to God. Injustice occurs when these people are left out, oppressed, or exploited. Justice occurs when they are included.

But too often we theorize about justice, forgetting that, for so many, justice is deeply personal. For the women of Congo, justice means peace. For millions of others, justice means overcoming war, escaping oppression, or eradicating hunger. "We know what justice is," said a group of Latino women during a conference on poverty. "It is bread for our children!"[31]

War, oppression, and hunger are symptoms, not causes, of something deeper: broken relationships. Relationships that have gone awry, have been ignored for too long, or are downright harmful—whether between people, villages, governments, or even the West and the Global South—lead to suffering and sometimes deeply entrenched patterns of evil as well.

When we approach the problems of suffering as relational, our response changes, sometimes profoundly. Instead of giving charity or aid, we will seek to strengthen relationships within a community, including especially the relationship of the vulnerable to the powerful, the local church to all ethnicities, and even the citizens to its government. As we do, we are mindful of the relationships between outsiders, which may be us, and insiders. While we may pursue our goals out of hearts of charity, the better way is through biblical justice. Only through relationships can justice be ultimately won.

When we live out justice in our relationships, we give witness to the person of Jesus and effect change. When we include those who are left out so they can become the hands and feet of Christ in their own communities, we empower them to bring justice to a suffering world. For a woman who cannot feed her child, justice comes in the form of a community banker offering a microloan or an agronomist teaching techniques to increase her crop yield. For a refugee, justice comes in the form of a hospitable heart and an open home. For the fractured community, justice comes in the form of racial reconciliation. Neighbor to neighbor. Tribe to tribe. The poor to the wealthy. The wealthy to the poor. Governments to their citizens. God to his people and his people to creation. These relationships, when stitched together justly, weave a tapestry of hope that can fundamentally change society for the better.

the heart of the matter

When we reframe the fundamental conundrums in the world as *relational* rather than problems requiring projects, we begin to see the need for the seismic shift I mentioned earlier. When the root of the world's problem is understood in this way, then everyone—and I mean everyone—possesses enormous power to effect change. The more willing we are to improve our own relationships as we work on behalf of those who are trapped in injustice, the better the world becomes. Our programs and projects produce lasting change because they are anchored in the right foundation.

A few years ago Belinda and I were speaking with a group of college students in Tyler, Texas. We discussed how injustice—human trafficking, poverty, racism, and war—relates to broken relationships, whether social, economic, political, or spiritual. I asked them to name the issues of injustice they were facing in their studies. But the room grew quiet. So I asked another question: "What is your major?" One student said, "Film." On the heels of his somewhat tentative answer, we started listing some well-known documentaries, from *Born into Brothels* to *Pray the Devil Back to Hell* to films on trafficking, the genocide in Rwanda and Darfur, and similar ones.

Then I asked, "How might you tackle injustice through the medium of film?" We explored the idea of using film to profile not only the problem but also the relational causes. As other students volunteered their majors—nursing, art, cosmetology, business, policy, you name it—we discussed the dominant justice issues in each, along with their relational roots and the possible solutions. Our conversation ranged from bioethics to genetically modified food to urban gardens and more. No one was left out.

When the impossible problems of our day are reframed, we change, because we see things differently. When we change, we find the courage to rise to a higher calling, redefining what we mean by *poor, poverty,* or *injustice* and rethinking the potential of those on the front lines of suffering. As we do, we pursue just relationships, where our calling joins God's grand vision, alongside others, especially those who've been left out for too long. Sometimes suddenly, but more often gradually, our age-old dilemmas start to fade away, and what we once considered to be conundrums begin to shed their clothes of impossibility.

SIX

when caterpillars fly

Help me to journey beyond the familiar
and into the unknown. Give me the faith
to leave old ways and break fresh ground
with You.

—PRAYER OF BRENDAN OF CLONFERT

I f the problem of suffering relates primarily to broken, nonexistent, or unjust relationships, then tackling root causes looks more like changing people than troubleshooting problems. Changing people, of course, is a very hard thing to do.

But it's possible.

Digging a well, for example, may not seem like an impossible task, especially if you know someone who knows how to do it. But helping the community value clean water is another thing. And hoping a community will share their new access to water with the village down the road or a neighborhood across the way is another thing altogether.

Consider another example. Pasadena, California, is home to more than 140 ethnicities. When a longtime Pasadena church admitted it was underserving its neighbors, it brought tears to the eyes of the Hispanics who lived nearby. "We didn't think they cared about us," they said.[1]

For this church, change meant first considering Hispanics as their neighbors, worthy of dignity and honor. Only after they experienced a shift in their values could they begin thinking about what could be done practically.

Reframing the problem from charity to justice, from giving things to empowering people, from an overemphasis on projects to an appreciation of relationships requires *all people* to change, including us, not just the ones with economic or social need.

"Change the world?" We hesitate. "Sure," we say with a hint of sarcasm, wondering why real change is so elusive. When we focus on symptoms, our efforts are futile. They will ultimately fail. But if we begin to understand and engage the root causes of change, something surprising happens, something remarkably valuable.

the anatomy of change

Deep down we long for positive change—in ourselves, in our relationships with family and friends, even with God. We believe change is possible when we pray, make a resolution, watch a film, write a poem, or lean into a righteous cause. We want to believe that good can triumph over evil, the underdog can win, and the world can be a better place. We live for change, even if we're afraid to admit it.

So why is enduring change so elusive?

One reason, I believe, is that we live as though change begins exclusively with thought. Whether we consciously realize it or not, we tend to put all our eggs in Descartes's famous basket: "I think, therefore I am."[2] We seek change first through a syllabus, a sermon, or a seminar. We give up when the rationale for change, or its benefit, doesn't make sense to us.

But does change primarily begin with thought? Can we really reason our way toward a better world?

James K. A. Smith, a philosophy professor at Calvin University, poignantly said human beings are fundamentally lovers. That is, we are *not* primarily "thinking things" or "believing animals" but rather "desiring human beings with a passional orientation toward the ultimate." It is a structural feature of being human, argued Smith: "We can't *not* be lovers. We can't *not* be desiring some kingdom. The question is not whether we love, but what we love."[3]

For Smith, Descartes's maxim would probably be reconfigured as *I love, therefore I am.* Or, perhaps better said, *I become what I love.*

So who's right? Descartes? Smith? Does reason trump love, or does love trump reason? Or should we agree with Aristotle, who said our habits ultimately change us, that we "are what we repeatedly do"?[4]

In the end Jesus trumps them all.

a tree and its fruit

"No good tree bears bad fruit, nor does a bad tree bear good fruit," said Jesus. "Each tree is recognized by its own fruit. People do not pick figs from thornbushes, or grapes from briers."[5]

With these words Jesus confronted the hypocrisy of his day. Just as in our culture, people pursued religion for show. They prayed so others could hear them. They gave to the poor so people would recognize their good deeds. Jesus was in effect saying religion is good only if it captures the full essence of a person's life, what he called the *heart,* and is proven true by deeds. If deeds do not flow from the heart, they are false. What may look like fruit is actually not. Similarly, if a changed heart doesn't produce changed actions, the heart hasn't really changed:

> Good people bring good things out of the good stored up in their heart, and evil people bring evil things out of the evil stored up in their heart. For out of the overflow of the heart the mouth speaks.[6]

An illustration of a tree and its fruit may help us understand what Jesus is saying.[7] What we consider true (our *beliefs*) informs what we consider best (our *values*) and determines what we do (our *behavior*). Our behavior produces what we see, whether good fruit or bad. In essence, Jesus was commending those whose *beliefs, values,* and *behaviors* work together in harmony toward righteousness, peace, and justice to produce good fruit. Genuine

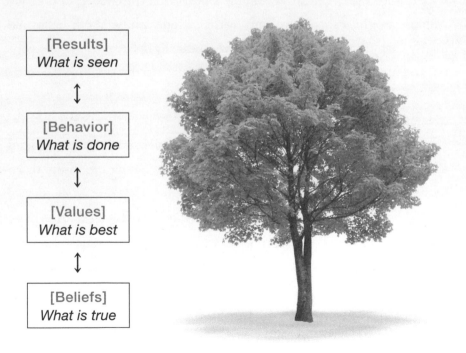

[Results]
What is seen

↕

[Behavior]
What is done

↕

[Values]
What is best

↕

[Beliefs]
What is true

change happens when all three dimensions are consistent, integrated, and resonant. Just as the roots of a tree must draw water to sustain life in the tree's trunk, branches, leaves, and ultimately fruit, so too must our beliefs inform our values and everything we do. And just as a tree's leaves must absorb sunshine to provide energy to the branches, trunk, and roots, so too must our behaviors affirm, and even *inform,* our values and beliefs. When such consistency is lacking, change is fleeting and short lived.

Too complex, or perhaps obvious? In theory maybe but not in practice. Most people don't realize their everyday choices are rooted in their value system and ultimately their beliefs. The reason the world continues to suffer is because so many good people unconsciously convince themselves they are helping when they are not or are not meant to help when they should.

We experience this phenomenon more often than we'd like to admit. Consider a roommate who promises to change after your heart-to-heart talk, but her change is short lived. Or consider the friend who talks about the importance of faith and deeds, even demonstrating faith in tangible ways, but justifies giving up when the going gets tough. In the long run the roommate's behavior doesn't reflect her promise because she didn't fundamentally believe that change was necessary. The friend exhibited signs of change but wasn't able to carry them out because his beliefs were fallacious or superficial; they didn't really impact his value system.

Or think about the follower of Jesus who justifies inaction because she misunderstands God's sovereignty, believing God is always "in control" even in the worst situations. She excuses herself because she believes "God changes the world, not us." Such thinking doesn't resemble Christianity but rather fatalism, a dangerous perspective, especially for those who suffer unjustly every day.

Why is all this important?

Understanding how change happens in our own hearts, as well as within local and global communities, is a prerequisite for diagnosing, sustaining, and multiplying impact. We can avoid superficial, short-term solutions by understanding what must change at a root level in order to sustain changes at the value and behavior levels. Or we can help trigger change by stepping out in behaviors that have the greatest potential to shape our values and shift our beliefs. The tree model helps us appreciate change, especially relational change, both within ourselves and within the communities we seek to impact. It speaks to reality, but it also dreams. It helps us discover *what is* but also helps us dream *what could be.*

Let's take a look at each dimension to understand how change happens, along with its implications.

beliefs: what is true

Our beliefs (the roots of the tree), composed of thoughts—both conscious and unconscious—are informed by emotions and feelings. Beliefs are usually handed down through generations in the form of culture and traditions. They include assumptions, or presuppositions, things that cannot really be proven, such as the existence of God, whether God is good or capricious, why we exist, and our purpose for living.

Belief is the deepest expression of who we are. It's the bedrock of our very existence. Even people who don't believe in God have a set of beliefs that are at the core of their being. Paul Hiebert, one of the most important contemporary anthropologists, refers to our core beliefs as our worldview, the "assumptions and frameworks a group of people makes about the nature of reality." Our beliefs, just like our worldview, are driven by more than intellect. "People think about things, have feelings about them, and make judgments concerning right and wrong based on their thoughts and feelings," said Hiebert.[8]

values: what is best

Values (the tree's trunk) determine where we put our time, our thoughts, our affections, our money. More than any other factor, values inform, guide, and activate our volition, our will. Hiebert placed emphasis on values, because they judge what we think, determining what is true or false and how we feel. Values can be rational, based in belief and principles. For example, I love my wife and sons; I value them highly. In fact, I consider them so important that I'd give my life for them if circumstances called upon me to do so.

But values can be irrational too. Addictions can warp values in ways that lead to choices that harm and destroy.

behavior: what is done

Just as our beliefs inform our values, our values inform "decisions that lead to actions."[9] Whether our actions (the tree's branches), and ultimately the fruit of our lives, are good or bad depends on our values and beliefs.

What does this mean for us?

When Jesus illustrated the authentic life by comparing it to a fruit tree, he was saying the person whose beliefs, values, and behaviors are fully aligned is a *true* person. When our minds and emotions, our reason and affections, are unified around truth as God intended it; when we value that truth so highly we organize our lives around it and live according to it; when we make decisions as if that truth were unequivocal, we are living a genuinely holy life. If, on the other hand, we espouse beliefs we really don't value and, as a result, act in ways contrary to our beliefs, we are living false lives. Jesus called that hypocrisy and its followers hypocrites.

When our deeds flow from what is most important, and when our values are anchored in God himself through radical, pure faith, we live what Dallas Willard calls "radiant" lives.[10] Living according to these principles is not only genuine and lasting, but it is outrageously infectious. It changes us and can't help but change others.

Remember, positive change will last only to the extent there is consistency along the tree. If alignment is weak, nonexistent, or contradictory, the change process will rupture or fizzle or never get off the ground.

the science of change

There may be no greater metaphor for change than the transformation of a caterpillar into a butterfly. We know there's quite a bit of science behind the mystery: a chrysalis, a cocoon, and conflict between old and new cells. Human change involves science too. Just like the butterfly, the tree metaphor helps us understand the relationship among our beliefs, values, and actions according to a set of principles. The tree functions as a tool to diagnose root problems and facilitate desired change within a community. It helps us reflect on the nature of change much the way a scientist analyzes a natural phenomenon or a complex process.

For example, many of us believe that God's image is stamped on every human being and that consequently all people are intrinsically valuable. Many of us also believe that Jesus asks us to love all people, including our enemies. We may hold others, even nations, to such a standard. But when someone offends us or brazenly takes advantage of us—call him an enemy of sorts—we may find ourselves contesting on the grounds of fairness or justice. We do anything but turn the other cheek. Why? Because we value fairness more than loving all people, even our enemies.

But how is this discovered? In a nonthreatening way the tree tool helps identify what we say is true and then compares it to how we actually live it out (or not). It tests our words against our deeds by grappling with what matters most to us, *our values*.

It can be used in simpler ways too. For example, my sons believe in God. And they believe God has called them to do something great, something world changing. But on some days what their friends say is more important than what God says. Following the tree logic, I can ask them to tell me how their words the previous day—when they spoke passionately about God and their desire to do good—work together with the choices they are making today.

We can also use the tree to understand what's really most important to us. For example, we may believe prayer is essential to a life with God. We may even believe prayer can change things. But we may pray only a few minutes a day, if that. Why? We believe in prayer but really don't value it. It's not that important to us after all.

Gradually we begin to see that our actions tell us more about our values than our stated beliefs. Our behavior, in fact, is a window to our value system. And our values tell us what we *really* believe. When we ask questions about our beliefs, we discover that intellectual awakening alone won't create sustainable change. And while emotional experience without the anchor of principled reason may lead to a temporary change, it will be short lived.

Understanding how root-level change happens helps us avoid superficial, short-term solutions. But properly diagnosing problems and understanding what must change comes first. Using the tree as a tool will help you diagnose broken relationships in a community, neighborhood, business, village, church, club, group, friendship, or an individual. It empowers everyone involved to discover and play a role in bringing his or her own change.

When you are ready to diagnose problems, follow the step-by-step process outlined in Appendix A, "the beautiful tree: a tool for discovering and designing change." When you do, you will discover how many people are willing and ready to change their world.

We know sustainable change is hard yet rewarding work if we wrestle with it and persevere. The right way is usually not an easy way. If it were, the world would already be a much better place.

I have yet to meet a person or a group who wasn't helped by the tree. Try it; I think you will be surprised. Its pathway is, in a very real sense, a journey toward freedom because we serve a God who promises not to leave us or our communities to ourselves:

> God's love for us is so great that He does not permit us to harbor false images, no matter how attached we are to them. God strips those falsehoods from us . . . because it is better to live naked in truth than closed in fantasy.[11]

Thankfully, God transforms our reason, affections, and will when we muster the courage to confront areas that need to change. To inform our reason, he gives revelation. To strengthen, shape, and guide our emotions, he communes with us during prayer, worship, and meditation. And to galvanize our will, he converts our feeble commitments into lifelong covenants.

We are not alone in our pursuit. "We have the mind of Christ," said Paul.[12] Jesus prayed for his followers to "be one" just as he was one with his Father.[13] And while the apostle Peter said he would lay down his life for his Lord, only to deny him three times, in the end God so infused Peter with courage that he gave his own life and changed history in the process.

SEVEN

a beautiful collision

It is from numberless diverse acts of
courage and belief that human history is
shaped.

—ROBERT KENNEDY

Understanding the anatomy of change and why it matters is only half the journey. How to trigger the process of change is the other half. Sparking change takes the God of the universe, a few imaginal people, and a beautiful collision.[1]

Consider a well-known story from the gospel of John. A woman was publicly shamed and surrounded by her accusers. A crowd had already lifted stones just as Jesus knelt to scribble in the sand. They had thrown the accused woman into a hole so she couldn't run away because they believed the Mosaic Law demanded her blood. They were justified, even righteous, in their actions.

So they thought.

Then Jesus cut the tension with a single sentence: "If any one of you is without sin, let him be the first to throw a stone at her."[2] Maybe the woman's trembling turned into sobs as the stones fell to the ground, slowly at first—

one thump, then two and three—then faster, until a field of stones, the collective weight of her shame, her guilt, her condemnation, lay strewn across the sand.

Or maybe she was so stunned she couldn't speak.

"Neither do I condemn you," said Jesus. "Go now and leave your life of sin."[3]

An unnamed woman about to die at the hands of her accusers was shocked by the scandalous compassion of God.

A beautiful collision.

This outrageous act by a carpenter-turned-preacher has echoed throughout literature ever since. In *Les Misérables,* when Victor Hugo's Valjean was caught stealing silver from the bishop who benevolently had given him a meal and bed, the bishop asked, "Why didn't you take the candlesticks too?" Overcome by the bishop's act of mercy, Valjean collapsed in an open field, his legs "buckling under him as though some unseen power had struck him down." For the first time in nineteen years, he wept as he grappled with the bishop's forgiveness,

> the most formidable assault he had ever sustained, that if he resisted it, his heart would be hardened once and for all, and that if he yielded he must renounce the hatred which the acts of men had implanted in him during so many years, and to which he clung. He saw dimly that this time he must either conquer or be conquered, and that the battle was now joined, a momentous and decisive battle between the evil in himself and the goodness in that other man.[4]

Valjean was confronted by a simple act of mercy and forever changed. Another collision.

A few years ago I met a woman in northern Africa who walked desert roads to a makeshift clinic. Her child, hungry for days, had forgotten how to eat. My colleagues in the clinic attended to her child with therapeutic feeding. As the mother watched, her child began to revive. She wondered aloud why my colleagues were trying to save the life of her child if, according to her religion, God had decided he would die.

By the time she and her child were ready to leave, the woman expressed hope. She had encountered a different God at work in her life. She walked home to a different world.

In this faraway place too dangerous to mention, an act of compassion confronted a woman's idea of God.

A beautiful collision.

We tend to think change comes through the slow dawning of an idea, the gradual understanding of truth, or the culmination of years of discipline. Sometimes that's true. But in my experience, more often change comes only after it has been *set in motion* by a collision, an act of outrageous compassion, a season of unforeseen suffering, or even a surprising offense.

Though deeply related, the nature of change and how change begins are separate and distinct. When someone's beliefs or worldview—her bedrock assumptions about life—are confronted by a person, a deed, or an event that doesn't reasonably fit within her assumptions, she has a choice. She can reject the event or the person as false, evil, or impossible, or she can stop and question her assumptions about life. If she chooses the latter, she must dismantle one or more beliefs, often beginning cognitively, through reason. A change in belief requires a hard look at her values too.

Questioning assumptions can sometimes lead to significant change. But questioning the bedrock of belief is threatening. The well-known sociologist Peter Berger said our perceived reality is "constructed by social consensus," creating a "sacred canopy"[5] of beliefs, some of which may be true and others false. What we sometimes consider to be absolutely real, foundational, even bedrock, may in fact *not* be. The problem is we generally don't know how to distinguish between what is true and what is false. This explains why good people can live for years fully committed to a version of reality later deemed egregious, ludicrous, or even evil. Consider, for example, how many in the last century believed in Nazism, Marxism, or slavery.

By reflecting on the tree in a different way, we can see how Jesus's teaching on bearing good fruit applies to personal and communal change. We can start at the top of the tree and work our way down to its roots. Some surprising deed, action, or result—a beautiful collision—confronts a value system and forces a reaction such as, *How can what is happening to me be fair?* Or, *That person is demonstrating a kind of love I've never experienced before.*

At that moment change is possible.

So when an event, an act of sheer kindness, or a situation of profound suffering confronts our beliefs, we can feel as if the very bedrock of truth is being destroyed before our eyes. Such destruction is sometimes essential for change to occur, even though it's far from easy.

Genuine change requires people to be bold, humble, and honest. It calls for radical courage to embrace the beautiful collision.

spark

If you resonate with this idea—the notion that something shocking, a collision of sorts, is usually needed to trigger the process of change—then you should ask a bold question: *Is it possible to spark genuine change in the life of another?*

In *The Cost of Discipleship,* Dietrich Bonhoeffer asked, "What does it really mean to be a Christian?" "For him [Jesus]," he says, "the hall-mark of the Christian is the 'extraordinary'":

> It is the life described in the beatitudes, . . . the city set on the hill, the way of self-renunciation, of utter love, of absolute purity, truthfulness and meekness. It is unreserved love for our enemies, for the unloving and the unloved, love for our religious, political and personal adversaries. . . . It is the love of Jesus Christ himself.[6]

Bonhoeffer then presented how this works in practice:

> The "extraordinary"—and this is the supreme scandal—is something which the followers of Jesus *do*. It must be *done* . . . so that all . . . can see it. It is not . . . some eccentric pattern of Christian living, but simple, unreflecting obedience to the will of Christ. If we make the "extraordinary" our standard, we shall be led into the *passio* of Christ, and its peculiar quality will be displayed [through us].[7]

What does this mean for us? When judgment is due, we lavish grace. When conformity is expected, we refuse. When suffering is acute, we give mercy. Through our hands and feet and words and deeds, we can choose to give, to witness, to demonstrate the tangible presence of God. All this can spark genuine change.

History is replete with examples where single, defining moments sparked change. On June 2, 1979, Karol Wojtyla, the first and only Polish pope, knelt and kissed the tarmac at the airport in Warsaw. Speaking to the largest crowd ever assembled in Poland—over one million strong—he didn't criticize the communist oppressors of his home country or call for a revolution. Instead he called upon the Polish people to accept a special role in the course of history as the witnesses to Christ's cross and resurrection. The crowd roared in unison, "We want God, we want God!"[8]

Noted journalist Peggy Noonan said, "It was [this] moment . . . that Soviet communism's fall became inevitable."[9]

Or maybe you remember the student who faced down the Chinese tank in Tiananmen Square in 1989 as an act of radical nonviolence, an image that still sparks change today.[10]

Less known is the story of a group of students from Youth With A Mission (YWAM) living on the border of Thailand and Cambodia in the late 1970s. They volunteered to clean out the latrine pits in an overcrowded refugee camp after the UN and other agencies had refused because they were so foul. But the young YWAM team jumped into the overflowing pits and shoveled until they were clean. Little did they know their deed would earn them the honor of administrating the camp and their story would become a pivotal moment in the history of YWAM as an organization.[11] One of the reasons Belinda and I left home for Africa years ago was because we heard their story. It was a beautiful collision for us.

We don't have to look far in the life of Jesus to encounter collisions: when he healed the guard's ear after Peter cut it off; when he dined with a tax collector; when he forgave a prostitute, telling her she would be remembered throughout history; when he forgave his executioners because they didn't know what they were doing.[12]

We can live the extraordinary life Bonhoeffer was talking about, sparking change in people through outrageous deeds, inconceivable forgiveness, unprecedented compassion. Whether our deeds are captured on Instagram or talked about in Twitter is up to God and the times in which we live. We need only to ask God for the courage to meet those moments when presented to us and believe our actions will spark the change we hope for.

imaginal people

Can we change the world? Yes, I wholeheartedly believe we can, and I hope you do too. But can we impact the *whole* world? Do we hope for too much?

"'Change the world,'" said Andy Crouch, "becomes shorthand for 'changing the culture at a particular time and place.'" Often culture changes us more than we affect it, but we can, in fact, influence culture by creating "cultural goods."[13] Crouch is right. And James Davison Hunter says our efforts to bring change can, in turn, spawn, shape, or renew institutions, churches, villages, neighborhoods, and even whole chunks of society.[14]

Sometimes we fail to see the ripple effect. Our choices can affect others, and their choices, still others. A critical mass of people can join together to affect whole groups, communities, and organizations, changing the culture within each. Rapid change can result and work to create *new* culture, whether in organizations, churches, schools, or neighborhoods, calling the individuals within these communities to a higher level of thinking, performance, and service. This dynamic interplay between individual and institutional change is an important one. The symbiotic relationship can make the difference between short-lived and enduring impact, as well as how many people are affected positively.

But institutions rarely create that first spark. Change starts with real people. People like you who dare to think differently, who risk, who care; people like you who bring the possibility of collision to a community oppressed by accusation, caged in faulty beliefs, or steeped in an unjust value system. Such actions can spark a movement, one that can be sustained through networks and institutions.

The scientific miracle that drives a caterpillar's transformation into a butterfly is nothing less than breathtaking. In her book *Butterfly,* Norie Huddle describes what happens at the cellular level. Inside the caterpillar the process of metamorphosis creates new "imaginal cells," which resonate at a different frequency than the old caterpillar cells. The old cells treat the imaginal cells as enemies and actually "gobble them up." But the imaginal cells continue to form and thrive.

Huddle describes what happens next:

> Cells start to clump together, into friendly little groups . . . , passing information from one to another. . . . The clumps of imaginal cells start to cluster together . . . a long string of clumping and clustering imaginal cells. . . . Then at some point, the entire long string of imaginal cells suddenly realizes all together that it is Something. Different from the caterpillar. Something New. Something Wonderful . . . and in that realization is the shout of the birth of the butterfly.[15]

This radical journey from defeat, even death, to "Something New" is a powerful paradigm. People who are bold enough to confront their own areas of change and, having succeeded, then attempt to impact the world usually struggle with feeling alone. They face rejection for appearing foolish, arrogant, or naive. Sometimes they're laughed at.

But when they meet other people like themselves—call them "imaginal" people—something happens. They cluster together, forming friendly little groups, resonating at similar frequencies, believing against all odds in the possibility of good no matter the cost. They hold on to their bold vision until something new is birthed.

If this is you, don't give up.

Short-lived impact is easy. It feels good for a season but lasts only for a while. Tackling the heart of change, at its root level, restructures how we see ourselves, others, and the world. And sparking that change through extraordinary deeds, those beautiful collisions, can become the first shout of Something New.

Part III

Remaking the World

EIGHT

begin the world over again

I saw an angel in the marble and carved
until I set him free.

—MICHELANGELO

S aving the world is not fundamentally about charity or justice. Something deeper drives them both. It has to do with God's strategy to redeem and restore the world. When we imagine a better world and discover
the mind of God, when we recover our mandate for remaking the world,
and when we tap into the drivers that spark and sustain change, we join a
divine pursuit that began with the dawn of time: the beginning of the
world.

Norman Borlaug was a farmer from Iowa. Born on the family farm eleven
miles outside of Cresco in 1914, he was of Norwegian immigrant stock and
baptized Lutheran. As a boy, Norman worked the farm, raising corn, oats,
cattle, and pigs. He attended a one-room school in Howard County until his
grandfather, Nels Olson Borlaug, encouraged him to give up the farm for the
city, saying, "You're wiser to fill your head now if you want to fill your belly
later."[1] Norman failed the entrance exam to the University of Minnesota, so

the school administrators offered him a spot in their newly created two-year General College instead. He financed his education by taking odd jobs, one with the Civilian Conservation Corps, which employed people during the Depression. Norman said, "I saw how food changed them. . . . All this left scars on me."[2]

While he was pursuing his undergraduate degree, Norman attended a lecture titled "These Shifty Little Enemies That Destroy Our Food Crops" by the soon-to-be head of the plant pathology department at the University of Minnesota. The lecture changed his life. Norman began graduate studies under Professor Elvin Charles Stakman and earned a PhD in plant pathology and genetics in 1942.

Norman developed semidwarf, high-yield, disease-resistant wheat varieties. (Yes, it's over my head too!) He combined these high-yield ideas with modern production techniques and introduced them to Mexico, Pakistan, and India during some of their worst droughts. Norman's wheat varieties thwarted massive famine. Mexico became a net exporter of wheat by 1963, and wheat yields nearly doubled in Pakistan and India between 1965 and 1970. A movement known as the Green Revolution spread across Asia as a result, and Norman's methods still inform food production across much of the world today.[3]

Norman Borlaug is credited with saving more than a billion people from starvation. In 1970 he was awarded the Nobel Peace Prize. In his Nobel lecture he said,

> By developing and applying the scientific and technological skills of the twentieth century "for the well-being of mankind throughout the world," [man] may still see Isaiah's prophesies come true: "And the desert shall rejoice and blossom as the rose . . . and the parched

ground shall become a pool and, the thirsty land springs of water."
May these words come true![4]

A farmer from Cresco, Iowa, imagined a better world and saved a billion lives.

Unlikely. Inconceivable. Impossible.

But true.

Norman Borlaug's story is a quintessential study in change. A biotechnology breakthrough, an agricultural revolution, and a billion lives saved. Borlaug changed the world forever; few would disagree. But it began with an encounter and a lament. In his own words the starvation he witnessed during the Depression—his collision—"left scars" on him. So he took a huge risk for his day. In an age when philosophers and sociologists were claiming the merits of natural selection and population control, when theologians and religious leaders were prioritizing faith above deeds, crouching behind faulty interpretations of "the poor you will always have with you,"[5] Borlaug dared to dream of a world without hunger. He chose to care. He committed his ingenuity to innovation, a technical "cultural good," a new creation. And create he did. Borlaug silenced the world's critics with a microscope and a petri dish. He defied all odds.

Behind the groundswell and the awakening, the sacrificial choice and the extraordinary deed, is something greater, more profound, and the driver of all change. It represents a first principle, including why we care, why we believe, and the basis of our hope for a better world. What is it? In a word, *creation*.

God created the world once, but he's doing it again. And he invites us to join him in the task. We are created to create. Whether he knew it or not, Borlaug participated in the re-creation of our world.

So can you.

created to create

In the beginning God created the world. But he was just getting started. The first creation, or *creatio prima,* as theologians call it, produced a formless, empty void. It was dark, wet, ominous, and foreboding. Its Creator "was hovering over the waters."[6]

Amazing, but hardly praiseworthy.

But the drama was only beginning. The second creation, or *creatio secunda,* took place over six days, beginning with "Let there be light" and culminating with the creation of Adam "in [the Creator's] own image."[7] The first five days were called "good"; the sixth was called "very good."[8] Out of the formless void, God created the extravagant world as we know it. From the stars he flung into space to the African crested crane soaring over wetlands, to the bloom of frangipane among blades of fescue green, to the joy lighting the face of a baby, no one would dare challenge God's magnum opus.

And then the curtain dropped on the second act. God stepped off the stage to rest; he took a well-deserved holiday, a day off.

But not before he handed the baton to Adam and Eve: "Be fruitful and increase in number; fill the earth and subdue it. Rule over the fish of the sea and the birds of the air and over every living creature that moves on the ground."[9]

God created Adam and Eve as image bearers and placed them in his creation for a reason. According to Reformed theologian Albert Wolters, God gave his people "a mandate to continue" what he had begun. The third creation, *creatio tertia,* began. God had formed and filled the earth, but it wasn't complete. According to Wolters,

> People must now carry on the work of [its] development: by being fruitful, they must fill it even more; by subduing it, they must form it even more. . . . [A]s God's representatives on earth, [they] carry on

where God left off. . . . From now on the development of the created earth will be societal and cultural in nature.[10]

God created you and me to create.

But what is our specific role when it comes to the ongoing creation? In Genesis 2:15 the creation mandate is restated, this time with a phrase that is helpful for understanding the word *creation*: "The LORD God took the man and put him in the Garden of Eden *to work it and take care of it.*"[11]

The Hebrew term for "work" means "to improve, refine, bring to the highest potential." It also means "to serve on behalf of others." To care means "to watch over, protect, preserve."[12] To work and to take care, then, suggests we are called to preserve and improve the world by *creating.*

But this idea represents only one of three Hebrew phrases that characterize Yahweh's mandate. A second phrase requires us to "radically improve" the world toward "perfection," and a third calls us to "perform unconditional acts of kindness, both person-to-person and also through structures, such as institutions, business, governments, and media."[13] The apostle Paul said it this way:

> Therefore, if anyone is in Christ, he is a new creation; the old has gone, the new has come! All this is from God, who reconciled us to himself through Christ and gave us the ministry of reconciliation: that God was reconciling the world to himself in Christ, not counting men's sins against them. And he has committed to us the message of reconciliation. We are therefore Christ's ambassadors, as though God were making his appeal through us.[14]

If we carve out creation from the story of history—indeed from even the meaning of history—or if we relegate it to gardeners and painters and poets and skip over entrepreneurs, caregivers, storytellers, scientists, technicians, mothers, professionals, and so on, we miss the point. We live desperate lives without meaning, and we leave the creation mandate unfulfilled. But if we instead

> see that human history, and the unfolding of culture and society are integral to creation and its development, that they are not outside God's plan for the cosmos, despite the sinful aberrations, but rather were built in from the beginning, were part of the blueprint that we never understood before, then we will be much more open to the positive possibilities for service to God in such areas as politics and the film arts, computer technology and business administration, development economics and sky-diving.[15]

But just any creativity won't do. It must be infused with the right values. We participate with God when we reflect his nature and character. When creative ideas and actions—whether scientific, entrepreneurial, innovative, artistic, or inspirational—are characterized by love, truth, honor, sacrifice, peace, and justice, they can permanently alter the course of history.

We are called to create with thought, word, and deed across the whole range of gifts and talents and professions. When we shrink from this call and fail to understand the blueprint that undergirds the mandate given to us, we disappoint our gracious God, miss countless opportunities to do good for others, and settle for shallow lives.

You are called to create with God, to preserve and radically improve the world, a process that begins in this life and continues to the next, a profound mystery we may never fully understand until God reveals it.

But there's more to the story: God also gives you the power to do it.

God wants to make you powerful

If placing the notions of power and creativity in such close proximity makes you worry, you have good reason. Years ago I came across a Dallas Willard lecture on leadership. He opened with these words: "God wants to give you power."[16] At the time I was grappling with the effects of leadership that had gone badly. I knew people who had started strong only to be compromised later by power. Power, in my mind, was something to scrutinize, if not avoid. We are all too familiar with the adage "Absolute power corrupts absolutely." History has a way of telling the truth: power gone awry is devastating.

For most of my life I understood power as the opposite of humility. St. Francis of Assisi rejected the power of the church by choosing to live as a beggar instead. Henri Nouwen stepped down from a prestigious position at Harvard to serve a community where people knew him only as "Henri."[17] I had stepped away from corporate ladder climbing to serve God. For me humility meant declining position and prestige.

But Willard was talking about something else.

Belinda says, "Power is the capacity to create *or* destroy." When we use power to create for virtue, for good, we are fulfilling God's "creation mandate," God's will on earth as it is in heaven. It seems Belinda understood Willard before I did.

In his book *Playing God,* Andy Crouch defined power as "the ability to make something of the world." I like his simplicity. He went on to say that power "is in a real sense the source of human well-being, because true power multiplies capacity and wealth."[18]

Virtuous power—the kind that "multiplies capacity and wealth," that is motivated by sacrificial love and selfless service, that lifts people from powerlessness—is a very different kind of power.

The God of all power introduces himself to earth in a nonspectacular way, with absolute vulnerability, a gentle whimper, and the fragile breath of a newborn. Who could conceive that the God of galaxies would step into the tender skin of a baby, shedding the glory he enjoyed in the heavenly realm? He didn't take up power as we know it. He didn't command from afar. He didn't force himself. Instead, he undressed himself[19] of ultimate power, joined human frailty, and camped among us.

Why is this version of power so different? Because this kind of power rests on humility. It's about who we are more than what we do and especially the positions we hold. It flows from authentic character, is motivated by altruism, and is accomplished through sacrificial love. It volunteers accountability because it's concerned about others more than self.

postmodern prophets

God wants to give you power, power to remake the world. But not all power looks the same. Our calling to create is different from one person to the next.

Several years ago on Mother's Day, I served Belinda breakfast in bed. Alongside scrambled egg whites and a sliced avocado, I slipped a newspaper with this headline: "Congo: The worst place in the world to be a mother." Belinda is an activist at heart; she often quotes British abolitionist William Wilberforce: "You may choose to look the other way but you can never say again that you did not know."[20] With a slight smile I said, "I thought you might just want to know . . ."

The article explained how moms in Congo were overcoming overwhelming odds to raise children in a war zone. They were unsung heroes the world had ignored for too long. I knew their story would somehow become Belinda's.

Belinda cried when she read it. She didn't thank me then, but she does now.

A little less than a year later, Belinda traveled to Rutshuru, the heart of a decades-long conflict in Congo, where mothers still *mother* somehow. The "superhero moms of Congo," as Belinda calls them, hold life together. Belinda visited an Internally Displaced Persons camp just outside Goma in eastern Congo. There she met Ayinkamiye, "Maisha," and her five small children in tent #B-27-47, an eight-by-twelve-foot white tarp, stuffed with straw in its corners to keep out water during the rainy-season deluge. Maisha and her family had fled Rutshuru two years before. Rebels fired shots in their village throughout the night, forcing her and her family to run. Their journey took three days under the cover of night. Maisha scrounged food along the way. "War came to our village," she said, "and we fled for our lives."

Belinda and Maisha, both mothers willing to give their lives for their children, prayed together in the dust and rubble of a protracted war. Despite their language gap and the world of difference between them, they understood each other as mothers do, at a heart level, a visceral one. After kneeling, praying, and crying together, they stood in solidarity. With irrepressible strength they gathered their courage—for Maisha to survive another day and for Belinda to tell the extraordinary truth about Congo's moms.

Creativity is often sparked by tears. Something is wrong, and someone refuses to shrug it off. These are the ones who vow to tell the truth, to do something about it. They complain; they lament. They call the masses to contribute to building something virtuous, something good. They open the door to creativity, a pathway toward something better, and they pave the way for others to create too.

They are postmodern prophets.

thank you for slapping me

The word *prophet* is rife with controversy. In ancient times if you were a false one, you were eligible for stoning. If legitimate, then you were inducted into history's Hall of Faith. Today, unless you are a rock band with a cool name, calling yourself a prophet will get you a scoff, a shrug, or at least a lifted eyebrow. A *prophet* refers to someone who delivers a message from God. Moses, Isaiah, and even Jonah were prophets. The word *prophetic,* however, is less weighty. It means to say something about the future God intends. The Bible talks about many people prophesying, not just a few giants:

> I will pour out my Spirit on all people. Your sons and daughters will
> prophesy, your old men will dream dreams, your young men will see
> visions. Even on my servants, both men and women, I will pour out
> my Spirit in those days.[21]

These sons and daughters are you and me. Are some of us prophets? In a strictly biblical sense, perhaps. But it's better to say that some of us have prophetic callings or, even better, that some people are called to stir up things for good, to tell the truth.

What is God's will for Maisha? To be free from violence? To feed her children? To educate her family? To walk closely with her Creator?

Absolutely. Yes and amen. All of the above.

Jesus is the ultimate example. He criticized the first-century problems not with war or weapons but with truth and compassion. Jesus offered solidarity with the marginalized—Gentiles, tax collectors, prostitutes, and the poor—by dining with them. He became poor himself, and in so doing, he validated their cry. But he also contested their suffering through healing and proclaiming a better way, a new kingdom. He offered ultimate solidarity through his death while also demonstrating a sort of divine protest through the resurrection.[22]

When we create with compassion, or justice, according to the will of God, we point people toward a better way: God's will on earth.[23] We reverse entropy—the tendency of everything, whether in Congo or at home, in a refugee camp or a decrepit neighborhood, to get worse, corrode, or erode. Being prophetic is calling attention to the will of God, an alternative way, to splash paint on the canvas of *what could be* or, better, *what should be*. It's a message from God to his people, plain and simple. For Belinda, it means telling the world about Maisha and the people of Congo. "We must do something so our sisters in Congo don't continue to suffer while we celebrate," she says. If one part of the human family suffers, we all suffer.

Think about these other postmodern prophets:

- the poet who laments the inner city
- the artist who paints portraits of peasants in Cambodia or Congo or eighteenth-century France
- the preacher who calls the bluff of false religion
- the architect who designs homes for the down-and-out
- the engineer who invents a new irrigation system for people living in sub-Saharan Africa
- the teacher who crafts the minds of children toward virtue
- the journeyman who fabricates metal or carves lumber to create something edifying
- the nurse who lifts the demeanor of a gravely ill child
- the sculptor who releases angels from granite or marble
- the mom who cares for her children in an overcrowded displaced-persons camp so they can smile

God's will? All of the above. Can you see it? God wants to give you and me the power to spark something creative, healing, helpful, honoring, or just simply *good*. When you do, you are creating something new, something true. You may be prophesying.

Postmodern prophets grab us by the ears and point our gaze to what is wrong. They cry; they lament. They create a vision of hope, an innovative solution, a better future. As a result, we begin to know too much about suffering to ignore it any longer. We are presented with the chance to join our creative acts with theirs and make the world better.

Belinda heard the cry of unsung moms, heroes from the other side of the world. She let their lament seep into her soul, and she chose to do something about it. If we are willing, we can listen too.

Thank you, postmodern prophets, for slapping us awake.

trailblazing the impossible

Creative people awaken others to do the impossible.

The founders of Mercy Ships, Don and Deyon Stephens, are friends and mentors. In 1978, at a public pay phone in Greece, Don Stephens negotiated the purchase of an eleven-thousand-ton Italian ship called the *Victoria*. He bought it for a million dollars. The sellers never knew Don's only office was a telephone booth.

Why a million dollars for a vintage Italian ship? Because a few postmodern prophets nudged Don and Deyon about the poorest of the poor in West Africa who had no access to health care, let alone surgery to cure glaucoma or strabismus or to remove life-threatening tumors. Mothers and fathers were going blind. Children were dying at alarming rates. So Don and Deyon began to dream about giving sight to the blind and life to the dying. And dream big they did.

Consider another dreamer, a trailblazer named Rose. Once a week, in Kenya, not far from Nairobi, just behind a local barbershop, a group of sixteen Kenyan women gather. Rose leads them in song. They talk about Jesus. They pray together. Then one by one, each woman places a few shillings of savings, often less than a dollar—usually earned from her business—into the group's lockbox. One or two women may borrow the equivalent of twenty to thirty dollars to pay school fees or the cost of an unexpected funeral or medical expense. Any interest they pay—according to a rate set by the group—goes into the group's pool of savings and benefits all the members. Each week they set aside a portion of their savings for a social fund to help their community.

On one particular day while leading the meeting, Rose burst into tears. She had been taking care of a family of orphans and was overwhelmed by their needs. That day her group decided to change its constitution so that a percentage of its social fund would go to support orphans within their community. And after one meeting the entire social fund was given to two older orphans who were also the sole caregivers of their younger siblings.

By most standards, even locally, Rose would be deemed poor. But Rose, like millions of others, is an entrepreneur. She helps her sisters save a dollar a week so their kids can go to school, eat more protein, and visit the local health clinic when sick. Rose is a theologian too and a practical one. As we struggle in our faith, especially with integrating "word" and "deed," Rose becomes a "little Christ" of word and action: she wears her faith on her sleeve. She's even apostolic, bringing life, the will of God, to others. As the world grapples with how to help millions of children orphaned by the HIV/AIDS crisis in Africa,[24] Rose takes orphans into her home. And Rose is resourcing her vision too; she is a philanthropist funding the welfare of others.

After the postmodern prophet comes the trailblazer, the everyday apostle, the one who is sent or set apart, the one who goes ahead. The trailblazer is the person who sees big, sacrifices large, and calls a thousand people to join her. Rose may be a hero few have heard about, but she joins thousands of others. They are the entrepreneurs, the innovators, the larger-than-life leaders, the ideators, the mavericks, the philanthropists, the mountain climbers.

Alongside the apostles, the entrepreneurs, and the innovators come the capacity builders—teachers, trainers, experts, technical advisors, pastors—who help us understand, who encourage, who landscape content and explain context so we can digest change, nurture it, and multiply it. Without capacity builders the vision can fizzle out or fail to achieve its intended goals. They make the impossible become *possible,* because they possess the knowledge—indeed, the wisdom—to anchor the vision into reality and nudge it toward full existence.[25] Without them the world remains unchanged.

a collective shout

Just like the imaginal cells of the butterfly, today's artists, innovators, pioneers, risk takers, innovators, and financiers find each other, sometimes at light speed because of technology. Together they create something new.

But technology alone generally doesn't provide the link. There is another breed among us: *storytellers.* These are the people who spread the news, the breakthrough idea, the new music, the story. They are champions, journalists, bloggers, preachers, and YouTubers. In his book *The Tipping Point,* Malcolm Gladwell calls them "Connectors," people who know lots of people, and the right kind of people, to foster an epidemic of sorts, a movement, the rapid spreading of something positive.[26]

If you are a storyteller, your message doesn't need to remain a lone cry for long. When your voice joins others, something powerful happens: hearts awaken, opinions shift, and people join. Your one voice becomes many, a collective shout, with the potential to change the world.

Friends of mine, Jenny Yang and Matthew Soerens—whom I affectionately refer to as the Frodo Baggins and Sam Gamgee of World Relief— sparked a movement by telling stories. Jenny is the daughter of first-generation Korean immigrants. She grew up in Philadelphia and experienced injustice against her family and community. Matt grew up in rural Wisconsin. Unlike Jenny, he didn't experience injustice growing up, but when he moved into a neighborhood near Wheaton, Illinois, his new Hispanic friends told him what it was like to live as immigrants in the United States. Jenny and Matt wrote a book to tell their story and portray a future vision, a biblical one, where God identifies with the least of these, asking us to welcome the "stranger" as if he were one himself.[27] Their "story" began with postmodern prophets who had long spoken out on a critical issue, then spread to people across the United States and into the corridors of Congress and even the Oval Office.

Jenny and Matt refuse to accept the world as it is. They are storytellers helping people find their voice. They are informing hearts and minds with truth, God's truth, and shaping national policy along the way.

I call that a collective shout.

When Belinda and I first met singer/songwriter Josh Garrels, we mentioned Congo. His response: "Where's Congo?" Less than two months later Josh gave away all his albums through NoiseTrade, a music-sharing site, to help the plight of women in Congo. Over 160,000 albums were downloaded, the largest in NoiseTrade history, and more than seventy thousand dollars was donated to charity. In his words:

When confronted with such a massive crisis that is in fact being
ignored globally, I was left with the overwhelming impression of those
in the midst of the suffering . . . being relatively "voiceless." And this
begged the question: if I've quite literally been given a "voice" to sing,

speak, write, and have some measure of influence in my own media-driven culture, why would I remain silent?[28]

Josh Garrels knows how to shout. And tens of thousands shout with him. Creation isn't done yet; God still creates, now, every day, straight through to the new heavens and earth as promised in the book of Isaiah. Whether through canvas or craft, inventing or implementing, building or administrating, blogging or singing; whether as entrepreneurs or pioneers, postmodern prophets or storytellers, teachers or trainers; whether on the front lines or back lines, young or old, educated or experienced; whether we fully recognize it or not, we are called to create.

passion, wisdom, vision, and the fellowship of friends

We often relegate creativity to artists, musicians, and poets. But God calls you and me to create no matter our bent, profession, personality, or skills. Participating with God in reconciling and restoring the world can be both exhilarating and daunting. If we choose to take seriously the message of Jesus, we must wrestle with his invitation to join him in re-creating the world.

It's important to recognize we are not all called to create equally. Because your calling is unique, your vision is unique too. A gift is not the same as a talent or strength, and just like talents, gifts are diverse. Any talent—whether artistic or analytical, left brain or right, linear or lateral—can be empowered by a range of intrinsic drivers, gifts that are part of your hardwiring. I've distilled them into four broad groups: postmodern prophets, trailblazers, capacity builders, and storytellers.[29] Each of these gifts can apply to any talent or profession. For example, you may be a graphic artist but are passionate about people who are forgotten. You are a postmodern prophet/artist. You may be a techie but thrive on starting new things. You are likely gifted as a trailblazer/techie. Or you may be a musician but a storyteller/musician.

When it comes to your purpose, often the commonplace areas in your life best inform what you are called to do. A practical process of reflecting on your life across a broad range of areas—your passion, wisdom, and friendships—can help bring clarity to your calling. And, as your purpose begins to emerge, you will likely find a picture of the future, your vision, emerging along with it.

Let's try this together. Think first about your passion, your emotional commitment driven by affections, motivations, or principles.[30] Consider the core motivations that capture your interests, the things that get you up in the morning. What drives you? What things do you pursue no matter how busy you are? What music? What art? What technology? What sports? What books? What films?

Consider your wisdom, your knowledge, and your experience, including areas God has redeemed through healing and forgiveness. Consider your areas of formal and informal study and also your hobbies and even arcane interests. Where is your knowledge base? What experience do you have? What fields of expertise? What discipline? What history? What issues? And where are your scars? Where has God redeemed you? In what areas are you healed or healing?[31]

Consider also your fellowship of friends—your social, personal, and professional connections, including your colleagues, students, and family. Include also the organizations or the networks to which you belong. Ask yourself questions as you reflect: *Where am I connected? What relationships are most important to me? How far do they extend? Do they connect along shared affinities or interests or by geographical proximity?*

As you ponder your passion, wisdom, and friendships, you may want to make a list under each. Once you do, consider highlighting words, phrases, and names that connect or relate or *could relate* to your calling (from chapter 3) and your core complaint (from chapter 2). Where do your passion, wisdom, and friends overlap with your calling and complaint? What are the natural connection points? Which ones jump off the page as you pray? Which ones stir something in your soul? What themes emerge? I've included my list below as an example.

Passion	**Wisdom**	**Friends**
Cycling	Africa	World Relief
Teaching	Economics	Accord Network
Running	Poverty	The Justice
Wife and kids!	Justice	Community
Photography	Culture	Facebook
The Most Vulnerable	Strategy	
	Storytelling	
Guitar	Theology	

Now consider fleshing out your vision—your picture of the future—using a tool called a mind map[32] to help you brainstorm in a visual way. Mind maps are created around a single word, phrase, or idea to which associated ideas, words, and concepts are added, radiating from the center.[33]

A *vision map* uses the concept of mind mapping to create a preferred picture of the future. When you have fulfilled your calling, what do you see? As you envision, ask yourself the *what* question before asking the *how* questions. Do you see peace in a village or neighborhood? If so, what does it look like? Do you see the kids on your street engaged in a whole different way, maybe taking on their own project to help someone?

To map your vision, write out your vision statement—or summarize it with a phrase that captures its central idea—in the middle of a blank page, and then draw a circle around it. Now review your list of passion, wisdom, and friends, and then start generating ideas:

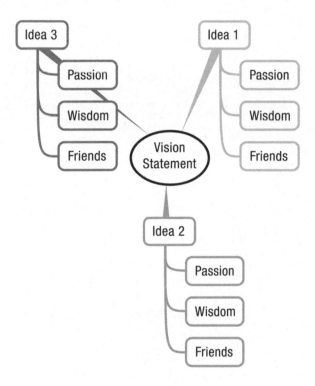

By way of example, I created a vision statement that is anchored in my calling, a picture of the future:

A movement of people bringing their wide-ranging talents, strengths, and ideas, from the artistic to the innovative, to overcome oppression and injustice everywhere.

Then I mapped two ideas inspired by this vision. The first involves engaging people in a more hands-on way at the annual Justice Conference. The second is an idea to engage my sons, Joshua and Caleb, in justice issues by applying their passions in a creative way.

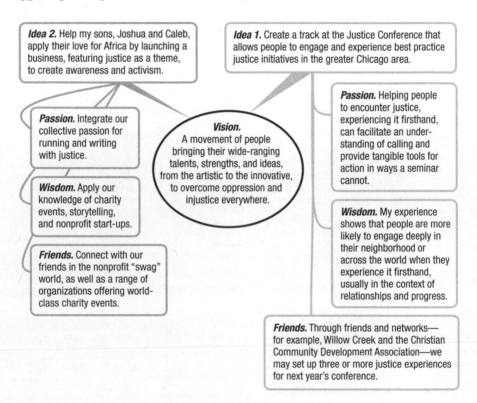

Idea 2. Help my sons, Joshua and Caleb, apply their love for Africa by launching a business, featuring justice as a theme, to create awareness and activism.

Idea 1. Create a track at the Justice Conference that allows people to engage and experience best practice justice initiatives in the greater Chicago area.

Passion. Integrate our collective passion for running and writing with justice.

Wisdom. Apply our knowledge of charity events, storytelling, and nonprofit start-ups.

Friends. Connect with our friends in the nonprofit "swag" world, as well as a range of organizations offering world-class charity events.

Vision. A movement of people bringing their wide-ranging talents, strengths, and ideas, from the artistic to the innovative, to overcome oppression and injustice everywhere.

Passion. Helping people to encounter justice, experiencing it firsthand, can facilitate an understanding of calling and provide tangible tools for action in ways a seminar cannot.

Wisdom. My experience shows that people are more likely to engage deeply in their neighborhood or across the world when they experience it firsthand, usually in the context of relationships and progress.

Friends. Through friends and networks—for example, Willow Creek and the Christian Community Development Association—we may set up three or more justice experiences for next year's conference.

a few shortcuts

If you are unsure how to discover your passion or wisdom, let me suggest two things—one relational, one practical. First, ask your family and/or friends what they think. Sometimes people closest to you understand your gifts better than you do. Second, consider taking one of the formal personality tests or strength assessments before you begin this exercise. I find Gallup's StrengthsFinder[34] especially helpful. While never definitive, these tools and others can shed light on your basic design from which you can then begin to assemble a more definitive personal blueprint.

Since passion and motivation are so closely related, let me say a bit about motivational theory. Daniel Pink, who popularized motivational theory in his book *Drive,* differentiates extrinsic and intrinsic motivation. Extrinsic rewards are well known—carrots and sticks, financial incentives, awards, and so on. Less known are intrinsic rewards such as purpose, enjoyment, or meaning in what you do. Intrinsically motivated people, according to Pink, "outperform extrinsically motivated people almost every time in the long run."[35]

The array of intrinsic motivations often complements certain personality traits. For example, someone strong in leadership—"Command" in the StrengthsFinder tool—will generally be more risk prone, more entrepreneurial, than someone who is strong in empathy or mercy. A series of simple questions can give you a glimpse of your core motivations, your passion, leading you toward a deeper discovery of your complementary strengths. Consider these questions:

- Do you like to uncover the truth?
- Are you exhilarated by starting new things?
- Do you thoroughly enjoy spreading new ideas or telling stories?
- Do you long to understand the deeper side of things?
- Do you thrive on accomplishment, getting things done?
- Do you feel deeply, even emotionally, for people when they suffer, and love to celebrate with them when they succeed?

Pairing motivations with personality strengths is an intentional step toward mapping your calling and vision or even just choosing where you should explore more deeply.

You may feel you don't have a whole lot of wisdom. But all of us have spent years in school, whether university, trade school, high school, or the esteemed school of life experience, to learn certain disciplines. Informally connecting your key motivators and personality strengths with your disciplines, and even your hobbies or passions—any area of learned skill—is especially helpful and sometimes quite surprising.

Belinda and I have learned a lot about ourselves through these simple steps. Understanding your passion, wisdom, and friendships against the backdrop of your calling and lament will shape your picture of the future.

In an ideal world you would commit your life to the area where your passion, wisdom, and friendships intersect. For example, if you are passionate about development economics, microfinance, or fair trade, you would ideally also have an MBA in business, finance, or banking, and your network would span both the academic and professional worlds, reaching also into the majority world. Or if you want to move the world through words, you would ideally have a journalism degree, experience with a major news outlet, and a passion to document how the world's so-called victims are changing their world.

But it rarely seems to work that way.

Most people I meet have an idea or budding passion about an issue or area of the world as a result of their complaint. They are seeking to extend their wisdom, or leverage-related wisdom, and broaden their network. But the operative words here are "extend," "leverage," and "broaden." They are not starting from scratch. I rarely find a visual artist or a musicologist who is interested in cocoa value chains in Ghana or Indonesia. And I have yet to come across an agronomist who feels called to hip-hop as a vehicle for turning the souls of urban crowds toward justice.

I've met many people, though, who feel they are in over their heads. If you feel incomplete, occasionally inadequate, or just plain insecure, you are welcome and in good company. If we had it all, we wouldn't need God.

Changing the world is tantamount to re-creating the world according to our calling, strengths, and vision, preparing it for a day when there are no more tears, no more pain, no more suffering. We are invited to create every day, no matter how grandiose or seemingly insignificant our efforts. God is ultimately the one remaking the world, but he asks us to join him because he wants to re-create through us. An extraordinary invitation for sure. What we do now, in time and space, remakes today and tomorrow and shapes eternity forever.

NINE

the making of heroes

Our culture has filled our heads but
emptied our hearts, stuffed our wallets
but starved our wonder. It has fed our
thirst for facts but not for meaning or
mystery. It produces "nice" people, not
heroes.

—PETER KREEFT

Charlene began her story with tears but ended with such a magnificent smile it transformed the room into joy. She lives in one of the world's poorest countries, one of the most dangerous places to be a woman and one of the hardest to be a mother. She told me how her husband was killed in the crossfire between warring militias, how she was violently assaulted by soldiers who were supposed to protect her, and how she fled her village with her eight children and walked for days. She forgave her perpetrators again and again until her deep wound was healed.

Charlene described how she joined a group of women to save small amounts of their own money each week. From her savings she launched a soap-making business. Over time she employed others and taught her sisters how to do the same. She also taught them how to forgive.

When Charlene walks into a room, she is honored with applause. She sings, she laughs, she keynotes at ceremonies. And, oh, can she pray.

Charlene is a hero making other heroes in one of the most difficult places in the world.

Across the ocean, in the early morning light, a woman throws her paddle into frigid Michigan waters. Lynne Hybels is close to completing thirty-six miles in a kayak to draw attention to the needs in the Democratic Republic of Congo. Lynne's family accompanied her throughout the day in power-boats, but her lone faithful kayaking friend had to quit because her kayak fell apart.

But Lynne didn't fall apart. After more than fifteen hours of paddling, half that against the wind, she finished at nightfall in dark waters to the glow of a distant lighthouse. In her words:

> Why am I doing this? . . . I am doing it as an act of identification and prophetic imagination. As I beat against the violence of these waves, I am beating against the violence that rips apart Congo. As I set my gaze against the wind, I am staring down the forces of evil and destruction.[1]

Lynne knew the women of Congo had been striving against great odds in deplorable conditions while the world looked on and whispered, "Impossible." So she kept paddling. Solidarity is love today—not then, not yesterday, but now. Real, raw, and painful at times.

Three years before, Lynne traveled to Rutshuru, one of the most afflicted areas of Congo. One of the first Congolese woman she met? Charlene. In Lynne's words,

Charlene did not speak quietly. She spoke on behalf of her sisters . . . with the strength and volume of righteous anger. She told us that victims of rape are often stigmatized with shame . . . so many married women refuse to tell their husbands they've been raped, fearing rejection and abandonment. But unmarried women confide in one another . . . and form a community of support.

We were all reeling from Charlene's story, but with darkness approaching we knew we had to take our leave so we could get back to our hotel under the safety of daylight. After praying with Charlene, we left her, but just as we reached our cars, she hurried to catch up with us. This time she had a tiny, two-week-old baby snuggled in her arms . . . her baby boy. She had been speaking not only of other women's pain, but her pain as well. She, too, had been raped. . . . In showing me her baby, she told me the part of her story she had not put into words. I was stunned with the overwhelming tragedy of her life, compounded now with the emotional and physical trauma of rape, and with a newborn to care for—in a setting where day follows day, and the only thing that changes is that each day gets harder.[2]

When Lynne was given a photo of Charlene three years later, she barely recognized her. Something had profoundly changed. Joy had outpaced her suffering. Love had won, hands down.

Lynne and Charlene are heroes, together making heroes of others.

But the making of heroes together is rare. Those of us in the privileged world may subtly think those who suffer are incapable of helping themselves or are, in fact, even responsible for their situation. Too often we focus on the wrong story, the story of victims rather than heroes, the narrative of impossibility rather than possibility. When we do, the real heroes are left uncelebrated and we remain unchanged.

where we went wrong

Over the last fifty years, the suffering of those afflicted by poverty, war, and injustice has become remarkably accessible. Media has played a major role in bringing the world's problems into our living rooms. Some of you remember the Ethiopian famine that we witnessed on the evening news. All of us remember the images of the tsunami in Asia and the earthquake in Haiti.

But we also know our culture is increasingly desensitized to suffering. As a result, the aid industry produces progressively shocking images and stories that feed expectations for more. We are caught in a vicious cycle, a dynamic that shapes our views about the people who experience suffering while overlooking others who suffer in less shocking but no less painful ways. People are dehumanized in the process, even without our knowing.

Sometimes what seem to be solutions introduce other problems. Take, for example, child sponsorship, where millions of children are supported monthly through a handful of organizations. Our awareness of, and connection to, those who suffer increased exponentially through child sponsorship. Some say child sponsorship is the most successful fund-raising innovation in the history of charity. After all, child sponsorship is a multibillion-dollar industry.[3]

Something special happened with sponsorship: people in the West began to associate faces and names with abject suffering. Rather than giving money in a disconnected way, sponsors were promised relationships with the persons they were helping. It brought human suffering into our daily lives. It taught us to care about real people with stories we could touch. Without such a tool, millions of people would not otherwise have engaged. Anyone could alleviate poverty for a dollar a day. Child sponsorship helped create a tipping point for mainstream engagement. For that, we must be grateful.

But the impact of sponsorship is controversial. There's an ongoing debate as to the merits and weaknesses of sponsorship as a tool for overcoming poverty. My friends who work in organizations that promote child sponsorship seemed to have figured out how to program sponsored dollars without destabilizing families or creating dependencies. When looking at the impact through the lens of education or child development, for example, child sponsorship is arguably a success. An educated child is far more likely to succeed than one who is not.[4] Even poor education is better than no education at all.

But when analyzing the impact of sponsorship from the perspective of empowerment, we encounter major problems. Sponsorship can undermine sustainable family- or community-driven solutions. We intuitively know that mothers and fathers, families, churches, and local communities are far better off when they can send their *own* children to school rather than depend on foreign charity.

But what about the impact on us? Far less attention has focused on the legacy of child sponsorship among the sponsors and the cultures in which they live. The success of sponsorship is built on the principle of scale. Sponsorship and similar innovations simplify, make bite-size, and commoditize suffering so anyone can engage. Maybe you have seen photos of children, generally forlorn, some emaciated, with a tag line that appeals to your emotions: "A dollar a day can save a life." But these photos can do more than foster guilt. They can condition us to see the poor as less than human. Studies show that the human brain reacts to such photos as if it is "seeing things, not people."[5]

It is through this lens, unfortunately, that most Americans and many across the Western world understand poverty. We see poor, helpless black or brown people desperately in need of help. As a result, poverty is dumbed down and the poor are often dehumanized, all while good, well-intentioned people believe they can be caring, world conscious, and ethical at a cost of only thirty-odd dollars a month.

And I'm sure you can agree that seeing people as "things" is likely to prevent us from considering their potential as heroes.

Ethically based consumer campaigns also tend to commoditize the poor. One example is the RED campaign, a celebrity fund-raising initiative to combat HIV/AIDS and other health pandemics in Africa. Why not leverage America's consumerism to tackle disease in Africa? To be sure, we are indebted to RED for raising awareness of one of the world's most critical issues. But have we reflected on the deeper costs?

Sponsorship, consumer campaigns, and the media's insatiable thirst for shock often transform our brothers and sisters into "objects of consumption."[6] (By "consumption" I mean the tendency to approach human need as buying and selling.) We feel better about ourselves not necessarily because the lives of those we seek to help are improving but because we so desperately want to *do* good so we can *feel* good. As a result, we may be congratulating ourselves as heroes at the expense of our brothers and sisters in the majority world.

In spite of the good things that may come from our best intentions, it's still too easy to believe our generosity is the only means for Africans or Indians or Nicaraguans or even struggling Europeans or Americans to survive. It's too easy to see these people as dependents with little power of their own. It's tempting to respond with pity rather than to treat them with dignity.

But those we may consider poor are capable of far more than just receiving aid. The right opportunities can provide a context where their innate potential will flourish. The right kind of giving can empower them so they can change their world. When they become heroes on their own soil, among their own people, so do we.

the wealth of the poor

Several hours' drive from Bujumbura, the capital of Burundi, sixteen women are changing their world. All are HIV positive. All have lost their husbands to AIDS. All care for their own children plus two or three orphans.

Today they sing hymns as they throw their hoes into clay-colored soil. They beam as they tell how they find strength in each other. They speak of their farming cooperative, how they earn income for their families and others. They pray spontaneously and with uncommon purity.

Few would call this meeting "church," yet in just a few minutes these sixteen women teach me more about what it means to follow Christ than any seminary course.

These sixteen are heroes, not victims. They are overcoming their suffering and giving hope to others.

Too often we tell the story of the victim even when we know all people are intrinsically valuable by nature of the image they bear and their God-given creative potential. But do we really *see,* and therefore engage, those who suffer according to their capacity or only according to their need? More often in our consumer-driven age, we measure people primarily by utility, production, or income. And that is dangerous for all.

To think properly about poverty, we need to consider the poor as wealthy too. Materially poor people around the world demonstrate vibrancy, human strength, perseverance, ingenuity, joy, and unprecedented faith. I've noticed that their dire circumstances and their "wealth" often correlate. For example, their virtue, character, and faith are shaped through suffering and trial. We have much to learn from these brothers and sisters.

In their book, *Building Communities from the Inside Out,* John Kretzmann and John McKnight differentiate between strong and weak communities:

Every single person has capacities, abilities, and gifts. . . . Strong communities are places where capacities of local residents are identified, valued, and used. Weak communities are places that fail, for whatever reason, to mobilize the skills, capacities, and talents of their residents.[7]

Identifying, mobilizing, and engaging the strengths of every individual are essential for any community to flourish. These principles apply equally to us, to our own families, churches, schools, and organizations. Without a biblical understanding of wealth in its full array—from divinely endowed gifts and nurtured abilities, to spiritual and social capital, to creativity—it's impossible to release the full potential of the materially poor to be agents in overcoming their own poverty and injustice.

reset

There is more to better thinking and good strategy in remaking the world. Hero making requires us to live out a certain set of biblical yet challenging values at the personal level. In many places of the world—from villages to neighborhoods to broader communities—we need to reset how we engage with one another.

In 1999 Belinda and I were living on a hospital ship in West Africa near Sierra Leone, where rebels were waging a horrific war. Young boys were being conscripted into rebel armies and forced to terrorize mothers, fathers, and siblings with AK-47s and machetes. We were helping friends, Moses and Sally, to evacuate the country. After weeks of difficult communication and careful planning, Moses and Sally managed to escape rebel-held Freetown and make their way to the Guinea border. On the way they witnessed an execution of a young girl. I'll never forget the moment they arrived on our ship. Sally collapsed to the floor and convulsed in tears. She thanked God for safe ground.

In the weeks and months that followed, first on the ship and later at a debriefing center near Geneva, our friendship with Moses and Sally grew. We shared life. We sang. We laughed. During that time I asked Moses to tell me how he felt about Americans, about the West, particularly about those seeking to help Africa. His first response struck me. He said, "You don't want to know." Some days later I asked him again. He agreed to talk after I promised him it would not affect our friendship.

What I heard next changed my life.

He told me that the West had the power, he did not; that Westerners speak, Africans listen; that Westerners give, Africans receive. He said Africans aren't allowed to question. They must accept whatever is offered even if they know it will fail. Africans smile, they bless, they honor. And he told me how Africans hurt when Westerners leave, because they never hear from us again.

It had taken me several years in Africa to develop a deep enough friendship for an African to tell me the truth. As Moses spoke, I listened. His words plunged a knife into my heart.

I repented that day, and from time to time I still repent for my unhelpful assumptions, hidden paternalism, and subtle arrogance.

Jesus connected fruitful living with repentance: "Produce fruit," he said, "in keeping with repentance."[8] Another translation says, "Prove by the way you live that you have . . . turned to God."[9] Sometimes our failure to repent is the only thing holding back a breakthrough, not just over there or down the road, but right here with us. So often the making of heroes begins with a simple reset.

we belong to each other

Once we reset a relationship, we are afforded whole new ways to understand one another.

People tell Belinda that she is a powerful voice for those who cannot speak up, that she tells a story that must be heard, and that when she tears up, they feel her pain and the pain of thousands more. "What can I do?" people ask in response.

Belinda exudes *empathy*, the "vicarious experiencing of the feelings, thoughts, or attitudes of another."[10] I believe this is why people are drawn to her. Empathy differs from sympathy or pity or even charity. It is vulnerable, selfless, and reciprocal, and it finds its best home in friendship.

Empathy puts flesh on compassion. It shows what we really think, how we really feel. It proves who we are. When we personally experience the depth of the love of God, when we conform to its ways, its unyielding nature, its stunning surprise, its astonishing simplicity, we cannot help but unabashedly lavish it upon others.

Empathy is a learned skill, not dependent upon certain kinds of personality, history, or expertise. Have you noticed that when you walk through seasons of trial, disappointment, or grief, you are more sensitive to others? That's because empathy increases with suffering. In other words, our own suffering becomes the fertile soil in which empathy germinates and grows.

Without empathy there is no making of heroes.

We belong, somehow, to our brothers and sisters who suffer. But do we feel it? Are we viscerally committed to their future? Are we willing to learn from them along the way, admitting our own needs in the process? Mother Teresa said, "If we have no peace, it is because we have forgotten that we belong to each other."[11]

You and I can become the kind of people who don't forget.

turning the tables

The values we are pursuing are important not only to the making of heroes but to anyone seeking to live differently. They are mutual, or reciprocal, because everyone has needs and everyone can become a hero. No one is left out.

On a Baltimore train three winters ago a man threatened to "blow my brains out." But a woman from Kenya saved me.

It was late, the cold air was sifting through to my tired bones, and my mind was preoccupied with conversations from a long day in Washington, DC. As I jumped off the commuter at Camden Yards to switch trains, the last leg before reaching home, I noticed a middle-aged woman dressed in a parka with a perplexed look. "Where do I catch the light rail north?" she asked with an East African accent.

"Come with me," I said. "It's about to depart. Can you run?"

"Yes!" she said as we started to jog side by side.

"You must come from Kenya," I said between strides.

"Yes, indeed," she said, surprised. "How did you know?"

"Oh, I couldn't mistake a beautiful accent like that!"

We exchanged a few more pleasantries as we boarded the train. She sat in the back; I sat toward the front. A minute later three men dressed in Orioles paraphernalia boarded the train and walked toward me.

"You stole my money," one man said to me.

"Oh no, it wasn't me," I replied with a smile, hoping to connect.

He cursed and sneered. "You've been stealing my money all my life, just like Bernie Madoff!"

Things unraveled from there. He let go with a stream of expletives followed by a promise to shoot me. The train was rolling now, so I had nowhere to flee. Whether he was gripping a gun inside his clothes, I didn't know, but in Baltimore it's usually a safe assumption.

Dropping my gaze, I began plotting how I could hold the assailants at bay until the next stop.

Then something amazing happened. The Kenyan, one of only two other passengers on the train, stood up, walked the length of the car, and sat down near me.

She said nothing.

For several long moments the three men scowled at us.

Then my assailant cursed the woman and turned away, and the three men strode forward out of the car.

It was silent now except for the rhythm of steel-on-steel and the distant voice of the driver announcing the next stop. I leaned toward the woman. "Thank you," I said.

A potential act of violence by people living a few miles apart in one of our nation's most dangerous cites was thwarted by an unknown hero from the other side of the world.

both/and

I've often thought about this experience. The woman from Kenya and I were both in need. She was lost; I was threatened. We offered each other help. Much to my surprise, our exchange became a shared one. We understood each other because we were vulnerable. We stepped beyond ourselves, she far more than I.

Both vulnerable, both in need, both able to give—a picture of reciprocity at work. The idea of reciprocity is an insight deeply rooted in the gospel. When Jesus sent out his followers to change the world, he told them not to take an extra shirt: "Don't take any money in your money belts—no gold, silver, or even copper coins. Don't carry a traveler's bag with a change of clothes and sandals or even a walking stick."[12]

Why? Wouldn't it make more sense for them to have an extra set of clothes, even a little money, so they could focus on more important things like healing the sick or preaching the message of Jesus?

One of the principles I have found hardest to learn is that receiving from those we seek to help dignifies and honors everyone involved. All of us feel valued when we can bring something to a conversation, a relationship, or a project, especially when we are in need ourselves.

The followers of Jesus had no choice but to ask for help. They had to eat. Their clothes had to be washed, their sandals too. In the midst of these miracles, the people were expected to give as they received. In fact, they were more likely to receive *because* they gave. Also, because the disciples were dependent on others for their very survival, they would not be considered godlike. Gods they were not, because they too were needy.

But how can we do this in our day-to-day encounters with those in need? When you are invited to pray, you can ask for prayer for your needs too. When you are offered hospitality, receive it and enjoy it. Listen to another's story. Celebrate his strengths, her culture, their creativity. Offer friendship and don't forget to follow up.

During our years in Rwanda, Belinda and I introduced a handful of fellow Americans to a group of African women. These women are part of an association that brings together widows and orphans to grow and sell high-value crops locally and internationally for as much as ten times the price of Rwanda's staple crops. Following our time together, an American named Cricket Barrazotto asked if she could pray.

I'll never forget what happened next. Cricket prostrated herself on the dusty concrete, stretching her hands to the feet of several Rwandan women. She prayed, blessing her "sisters, who deserve honor, who are loved by our Creator, who teach us, who inspire us."

Then she asked the Rwandans to pray for us. We bowed our heads, some of us kneeling, others beginning to cry as the women prayed.

In one small act Cricket leveled the differences between "us and them." Though we were rich in their eyes, she asked for prayer. Though we were received as kings and queens, she prostrated herself before them as a servant. Though they thought we had everything, she asked for help.

Recognizing we need change as we bring change is essential. Genuine, two-way relationships create an ideal context for the change we seek. Heroism is blind to status, power, privilege, and color, and heroes are made in earthy trenches more than on privileged platforms and in our daily choices to serve someone else with courage and vulnerability because we see the hidden potential, the poignant opportunity, or the pregnant victory.

The making of heroes is indispensable to remaking the world. Once we see the potential of others and experience their joy when they impact their world, there's no going back to the old ways. But we have to live it too. Simple humility and authenticity, anchored in trusted relationships, afford us the freedom to repent when we need to, to offer genuine empathy when required, and to receive both in return.

When we make heroes, we become heroes too.

TEN

hatching hope

Everything that is done in the world is
done by hope.

—MARTIN LUTHER

Making heroes out of unexpected people is an audacious task because most believe it's impossible.

Except for the heroes themselves, of course.

When we experience something inspiring, influential, and tangible springing up from unlikely people, we become believers in a different kind of change, a surprising change brimming with potential to multiply to thousands.

I experienced this kind of change a few months ago while visiting Rwanda. Five Rwandese pastors, representing a broad cross section of faith traditions, told me about seventy-five other pastors, all working within their communities to help families save and borrow from one another to start businesses, send their kids to school, and put protein on the table more than once or twice a year. Our role as an outside organization was focused on apprenticing communities toward a district-wide community banking initiative.

After the pastors shared a handful of poignant stories, one of my fellow visitors asked, "What's different about our work compared to that of all the others working in Rwanda?"

Their answer was stunning. After deliberating among themselves for two or three minutes, they paused before giving their answer: "You are different because you don't give us money!"

After a pregnant pause they burst into laughter.

And so did we.

Amid the laughter, deep inside I couldn't have been more pleased. I wanted to celebrate their success. These pastors showed how their change came from among their own people, within their communities and the churches they led. And they were deeply honored by it. We had successfully midwifed their honor by catalyzing the potential of their leadership and their people.

Rare? Yes, I suppose it is. Charity is still too often reduced to giving from the outside rather than mobilizing resources from within.

But these heroes were demonstrating something far more than just a different version of doing good. They exuded a refreshing joy, an uncommon dignity, and a deep ownership of their progress. Above all, I sensed an overwhelming *hope* for the future, not just for themselves, but also for the people they represented.

what makes heroes

Heroes don't just happen; they are made. A shift in how we view change, a commitment to better ideas and practices, and the right opportunities are all necessary. But one thing undergirds them all: *hope*. The idea and practice of hope is so central to change, yet we often miss it or take it for granted.

When we think of Jesus, we often think of love or faith or truth. Yet his indelible impact on people, especially the down-and-out and disenfranchised, was invariably *hope*. When Jesus encountered the blind, lame, sick, deaf, or dead, they left seeing, walking, healthy, hearing, and alive.[1] When Jesus talked about the pathway to God, the thirsty, mournful, pure, merciful, and meek left with a spring in their step—maybe even a gallop.[2] When Jesus dined with prostitutes, tax collectors, and other riffraff, their lives turned upside down because they encountered a divine hope they had all but written off.

The only people who didn't leave hopeful were the selfishly proud, pious, and powerful. To the rest of the crowd, Jesus imparted something uncommon, something big enough to start a reformation. He simply electrified his audience.

Was it his words? his charisma? his supernatural power? Maybe all three. But it was practical too.

In the opening pages of the gospel of Luke, the peasants of the day searched out John the Baptist, the forerunner to Jesus. He told them about a Messiah who would inaugurate an era unlike any other, not just for the elite but for everyone. He invited them to repent and believe. And he baptized them in the river to seal the deal.

But they didn't know what it meant for their daily lives. So they asked, "What should we do?" John responded by telling them to "share with the one who has none."[3] With these words John inaugurated a better pathway to charity and justice based on the prophets of old. He set a precedent for ages to come.

What is stunning is this: the people he was preaching to were not the elite, the wealthy, or even the middle class. They were the ragamuffins of his day. When the people who were barely getting by asked the forerunner of Jesus how to live, he offered a lecture in ethics in about twenty words: "If you have two shirts, give one to the poor. If you have food, share it with those who are hungry."[4]

If the idea of charity or justice were predicated on wealth or status, these people would have laughed at John's answer. But they didn't laugh, and John wasn't playing a cruel joke. Instead, John was calling them to something far more important than charity. He saw in their faces the image of God and, along with it, their potential to meaningfully change their world. When he asked them to give—even out of their need—he affirmed their dignity and invited them to make a difference. In a few words John effectively said, "If *you* have hope, you must give it to others too."

In one fell swoop he invited the poor to become heroes.

For anyone willing to genuinely give, that is, to believe in the value and possibility of generosity—especially for those who have so little—he or she must expect a better future and one that is also attainable. Belief in something good must be anchored in a higher reality, a reasonable expectation that goodness will in fact happen.

In a word they must have hope.

When John told people to share, he was asking them to believe in something better, not just an abstract idea, but a real and tangible here and now, for one another.

John was calling them to hope.

"*Everything* that is done is done by hope."[5] Is Luther's boldness warranted? Could it be that simple?

If we define hope as "the desire of some good with the expectation of obtaining it" or "the confidence for something better"[6]; if our faith undergirds all hope; if it is "the assurance of things hoped for"[7]; and if Christ is *in* us, "the hope of glory,"[8] then hope is a prerequisite for any thought, inclination, or action that seeks to make the world a better place.

Put simply, in order to seek change in the world, one must believe in hope. Hope is the engine that drives all change. It's the flame inside the furnace, the spark that fuels passion, the embryo of growth, and the gumption behind action. Hope is where it all begins, the very substance of anything we label progress. Without hope, we cannot make the world better.

more than a penny and a drop

The most amazing thing about hope is that it belongs to anyone willing to believe and to risk putting action to belief. No one is left out; no one is too poor or too weak to hope. Remember the story of the widow's mite?

> Jesus saw the rich putting their gifts into the temple treasury. He also saw a poor widow put in two very small copper coins. "I tell you the truth," he said, "this poor widow has put in more than all the others. All these people gave their gifts out of their wealth; but she out of her poverty put in all she had to live on."[9]

The widow had every reason in the world to skip the offering plate. Widows in the first century were economically and socially nonviable. Yet she gave out of her poverty as an act of courage, creativity, and even worship.

But why did she do it? Because she believed goodness would visit her despite her circumstances. And she believed she could have a hand in bringing goodness to others too. She lived her life on the premise that God was good and he was going to make the world a better place.

In a word, she had hope.

There's another story in the Bible about a widow who took a risk:

> The wife of a man from the company of the prophets cried out to Elisha, "Your servant my husband is dead, and you know that he revered the LORD. But now his creditor is coming to take my two boys as his slaves."

Elisha replied to her, "How can I help you? Tell me, what do you have in your house?"

"Your servant has nothing there at all," she said, "except a little oil."

Elisha said, "Go around and ask all your neighbors for empty jars. Don't ask for just a few. Then go inside and shut the door behind you and your sons. Pour oil into all the jars, and as each is filled, put it to one side."

She left him and afterward shut the door behind her and her sons. They brought the jars to her and she kept pouring. When all the jars were full, she said to her son, "Bring me another one."

But he replied, "There is not a jar left." Then the oil stopped flowing.

She went and told the man of God, and he said, "Go, sell the oil and pay your debts. You and your sons can live on what is left."[10]

On the heels of asking how *he* could help a widow in despair, the prophet Elisha asked *her* what *she* had to offer him. Nothing at all, she told him, underscoring her desperation by pointing to the few drops of oil in her kitchen.

But Elisha seized the moment. He saw the opportunity hiding in her need and empowered her to do something with it. A miracle happened when she gave out of her want to fill her neighbors' jars with oil.

She gave something. She did something. Why? Because she chose to believe in a better future; she chose to hope. And her willingness made her a hero among her friends.

The poor may be desperate, their strengths and abilities insufficient, but they are not victims. Heroes, like this widow long ago, *hope*.

hope, plural, and bottom up

"The opposite of poverty," said theologian Jürgen Moltmann, "is not wealth, but community."[11] Really? The antidote to poverty—and for that matter, one could argue, oppression and injustice too—is *community*?

You may be convinced that Jesus is interested not only in saving people but in saving the world too. His strategy, then, is focused not only on the individual but also on whole communities. The church is essentially not about a building, a liturgy, or a service but about a community of faith offering worship to God and help to others. The church's central message, the gospel, "in all its fullness," says Lesslie Newbigin, "introduces the vision of a new world, a different world, a world for which it is legitimate to hope."[12]

The gospel gathers a community toward worship and in so doing lays a foundational set of values to sustain the community beyond itself. It orients the community toward others. It breeds hope.

The gospel calls forth concrete action *for the community* from *within the community*; it is an intrinsic call, one that is essential to sustain hope. The gospel challenges the status quo to think differently, sometimes radically, while honoring everyone in the process.

With so much potential, talent, and capacity in the majority world and the need to focus on serving those who are closer to the problems, those who must lead their families, churches, and communities to their better future, we may ask, "Should we step back altogether?" Shouldn't those of us in the so-called developed world leave the needed changes to those closest to suffering?

The short answer is no. The better question is, what role must we play?

The theology of the body of Christ, *Corpus Christi,* helps us see the big picture. From God's perspective unity and diversity go hand in hand; everyone is essential, the entire body. To exclude Rwandans or Cambodians or

Latinos or Bolivians or Romas or Americans or women is to fail. We need each other. We must find unity in Christ to discover our diversity, that essential contribution each of us has to offer.

We can learn how to hope better together than alone. Have you ever experienced hope in unexpected places? I've found that hope is sometimes strongest where the need is greatest. We need hope just as much as those closer to suffering. They can, in fact, become our greatest teachers.

Even still, we might ask, if there is so much capacity locally—"wealth," as I call it—then why must we keep helping? Focusing on the strengths of communities does not mean these communities don't need our partnership. The strengths of individuals and local communities are indispensable, but they may not be fully sufficient. Outside resources will be effective only if the local community is mobilized and invested. When we fail to engage locally first, the results can be costly. Rowen Williams said:

> Attempts to bypass local networks, local styles of decision-making, and above all local rationales for action or change invariably produce resentment and puzzlement. What people see is an agenda that is not theirs, activated by foreigners claiming to act on their behalf. . . . If development processes and programmes are not to be paralysed by such resentment and mistrust, with the result that local communities cannot see themselves as agents of their own change, enormous potential is left unrealised.[13]

When we seek change together, as a global community, everyone benefits. Change from the inside out emerges from a foundation of hope where everyone believes in goodness, not just for some but for all, and where each person is called upon to contribute to a better future. Such a vision honors, includes, and empowers. And in the end it's the only kind of change that matters.

manufacturing hope

But maybe you consider hope to be too abstract or serendipitous or even capricious. All this may sound exciting and even inspirational but not necessarily practical.

So what if I were to say that the first step toward creating sustainable change is to create hope?

When individuals and communities become agents of their own change, something powerful happens. It is the key to sustainable change. But how do we ensure such change? By manufacturing hope.

In *Pedagogy of the Oppressed,* Paulo Freire spoke to raising the consciousness of the poor as a means of restoring their identity. Using literacy as his context, through a process of "critical discovery," action, and reflection, Freire helped people understand who they were, moving them from being mere *objects* to being *subjects* in the world around them. Significantly, the community chose its own educational content. During this process of discovery, "peasants, urban slum dwellers, simple fishermen, artisans, and housewives reflect, often with a sense of awe, on their achievements."[14] Dignity and self-worth and hope increase. Choice and freedom are discovered, often for the first time.

Many have dismissed Freire over the years for his association with liberation theology and even Marxism.[15] Liberation theology has led some to take up arms and adopt Marxist ideas. Wrong and deeply unfortunate for sure. But the heart of Freire's method is worth redeeming. When done well, its essence can reflect the heart of the gospel, offering people purpose, hope, and a pathway toward recognizing their God-given identity and potential. Nicholas Wolterstorff, of Calvin College and Yale, acknowledged Freire's theories of education but proposed a better basis for his work. Wolterstorff said the "right ordering of our relationships—with God, with society, with nature, with the legacy of human culture, and yet, with oneself" is the theological and philosophical basis for change.[16] Sounds like justice, doesn't it?

Applied with a biblical perspective, Freire's method can be a practical means of restoring hope among people who have been marginalized by poverty or oppression, often over a lifetime. Such awareness can lead to a restored identity, which is essential for releasing the potential of those who consider themselves victims. Their restoration helps them become agents in their own transformation and also the transformation of relationships within a community. Without such consciousness, or self-efficacy, they may merely continue to "accept the passive role imposed on them."[17]

Certain practical tools can help us manufacture hope among people who have traditionally seen themselves as objects or even victims. Such tools seek to facilitate change from the perspective of strengths rather than needs. Together with the community, they seek to create hope, depending on God, of course, to impart it to his people.

Of these tools, *appreciative inquiry* is the most common. It looks at a glass as half-full rather than half-empty, leveraging strengths or assets to overcome weaknesses. Helping someone top off a half-full glass is an entirely different project from pointing out why it's half-empty. If you've ever come up short—words that fell flat, an idea that just didn't bloom, or a project that petered out—or felt you weren't good enough, you know what I mean.

In a very real sense, the principles of appreciative inquiry can be used in everything we do, from overcoming personal challenges to raising children to overcoming conflict to saving the world. Rather than starting with needs or problems, beginning with strengths lays a foundation for long-term success.

Focusing on the gifts, abilities, and capacities of individuals and communities to solve problems shows that we really do believe in the heroic potential of those we are trying to empower. When we do, we trust them. And trust engenders hope.

Asset-based approaches represent an inside-out process with the purpose of outside resources being to identify, catalyze, and mobilize insiders to work for their own change. Identifying and mobilizing the capacities of people also help the community to produce its own agenda or, at a minimum, a shared agenda. Local ownership becomes the foundation and mechanism for sustainable change.

Appreciative inquiry considers people's intrinsic strengths as immensely valuable. Social capital, the "collective value" found in relationships, can provide the foundation for wide-scale community change.[18] Another latent strength, spiritual capital—the resource or benefit to an individual, group, or organization that arises from belief in God—along with prayer and other practices associated with faith can exponentially release human potential.

The practice of mapping strengths, which is usually called asset mapping, has the potential to launch an entirely new trajectory in a community. It's the art (and science) of manufacturing hope. It may begin with an individual or just a few friends, but it can snowball into powerful change—change that is driven from the inside out, change that invigorates and lasts. I've seen it firsthand. It's inspiring and powerful, the substance of hero making. Mapping can mobilize and empower hundreds, even thousands and millions, to multiply change.

Appendix B, "mapping a better future: a tool for mobilizing, implementing, and multiplying change," includes a step-by-step mapping tool. It builds upon the tree tool to foster change in your neighborhood, village, church, school, business, group, or community. I trust you will find it to be a practical application of all we have been pursuing together.

completely, entirely, and utterly hope

My friend Bill Haley leads a retreat center in the Shenandoah Valley called Corhaven. He says the way to know if someone is successful is to evaluate a person's life a hundred years after he or she is gone.

What perspective.

Will the vision you and I pursue today bear fruit for a hundred years or more after we die? Will it generate sufficient hope in those around us to sustain change for more than a hundred years?

Sometimes we think of hope only in future terms. But hope has already begun. On the corner of the spacious green in Boston Common, you will find a monument to the discovery of ether as an anesthesia in 1846. There are two Bible verses on either side of the stone edifice. One, from the book of Revelation, reads, "Neither shall there be any more pain," and a second, from Isaiah, reads, "This also cometh forth from the LORD of hosts, which is wonderful in counsel, and excellent in working."[19]

We know the biblical narrative assures a hopeful end to history: "He will wipe every tear from their eyes. There will be no more death or mourning or crying or pain, for the old order of things has passed away."[20] God boldly promises human flourishing at the end of all time. We know suffering will *not* finally stop until the end of history as we know it, until "the old order" has been replaced with the new.

But we also know the end of suffering has already begun. Consider how many tears have been spared by anesthesia. Do we have William Thomas Green Morton to thank? Or what about penicillin? Think of the millions of lives saved by the serendipitous discovery of a special kind of mold! Do we have Alexander Fleming to thank? Or are these merely whispers, signs of hope, visions given to people, accidental and otherwise, from the God of the universe, the One who creates and then creates again? Is he not asking unsuspecting heroes, ragamuffins though we are, to join in his great project if we are only bold enough to try, courageous enough to be honest, tenacious enough to walk the long line, and humble enough to create heroes in others rather than seek fame for ourselves?

Our flourishing has already begun.

And hope is inextricably linked to our vision—hope for a better *then*, a hope we can taste *now*. Should hope be available to only a few as those living in the corners of the world look on in desperation?

I don't think so.

Last year Belinda and I traveled to the Pacific Northwest for a series of engagements over a long weekend—events at a college, at a university, and in the local community. The aspens were just beginning to turn fire yellow. The air was crisp, and the mountains were already snow capped. It never takes much prompting to say yes to traveling west.

Longboards, wheels tipped up, lined the hallway leading to the college auditorium. The room was filled with bushy beards, knit hats, and boisterous chatter. The mood was tempered until I started telling stories. "We know too much today," I said. "Your generation refuses to turn away from the world's suffering. You can do something about it." I closed with a top-ten list of what they could do now. Those in the auditorium rose to the challenge.

After the meeting I dove into a handful of conversations. Belinda did too. After ten or fifteen minutes, I remembered I had a scheduled call, so I made a beeline for my car. On my way I stepped into a conversation Belinda was having. As I did, I was struck by the glowing beauty of the woman Belinda was talking to. I said something I've never said before, something I would never say unless Belinda was present: "You have a beautiful face." Then I ducked out, making my way to the parking lot.

Thirty minutes later, just as I was finishing the call, Belinda joined me in the car. She said, "Do you have any idea what you did to Jennifer, the woman I was talking to?"

I responded with confusion. "I thought I told her she had a beautiful face."

"Yes, you did," said Belinda. "But when you walked away, she buried her face in her hands and began to cry."

Belinda consoled Jennifer, embracing her as she cried. When she composed herself, she told Belinda her story. On a snowy winter night when she was only four, Jennifer's red jumper caught fire when she brushed against a candle in her home. The fire quickly spread to her long hair, engulfing her back and threatening her neck and face. Jennifer's mom and sister quickly rolled her on the floor to smother the flames. They called 911.

Belinda noticed the pale scars just under Jennifer's collar as she spoke. Through her sweater Belinda could feel the scar tissue on the Jennifer's arm.

Jennifer continued. She lived in a small rural town, ill-equipped to handle burn emergencies. The snowstorm made an emergency flight impossible. Her mom sat with her as the ambulance drove eighty-nine miles to the nearest major city. The paramedics gave Jennifer oxygen with an adult-sized mask. They couldn't give her an IV because they didn't have a pediatric needle. Jennifer's body began to turn, in her words, "a frightful gray color" that made its way across her shoulders, neck, and up her face toward her nose. The paramedic told the driver to hurry because time was short.

But what should have taken ninety minutes took four hours due to the storm.

When they finally arrived the hospital, a team of two doctors and eight nurses spent four hours saving her life. She had lost so much fluid it took almost two hours to administer an IV. Once she was stabilized, they applied burn cream across her body and moved her to a temperature-controlled room to prevent infection.

Two doctors, a pediatrician and a reconstructive surgeon, met Jennifer's mom in the waiting room. They said her daughter had experienced second- and third-degree burns across most of her torso, her left arm and hip, and her chin and left ear. They offered little hope. The surgeon told her to go home and prepare for the death of her daughter.

Days turned into months. Her mom donned surgical clothing to visit Jennifer each day in the hospital. She sat by her daughter's bedside, helping the nurses with basic care. She longed for any good news, hoping for a breakthrough. The doctors promised they were doing everything possible, but the surgeon maintained she needed to prepare herself for Jennifer's death.

Then Jennifer told Belinda something stunning. "Toward the middle of the third month in the hospital, Jesus came to visit me." Like every other day her mom had come into her room dressed in surgical gear. But that day she had been crying. Jennifer told her mom she had "a message from Jesus." She described how Jesus had visited her, that he put his hand on her forehead and prayed for her. And then she relayed his message to her mother. "You don't have to cry anymore because I am going to be okay. I am going to live," she said.

A month later Jennifer left the hospital for home.

In the coming months and years, Jennifer underwent a series of reconstructive surgeries, too many to count. Today she is married, has children of her own, and through World Relief teaches fiber arts (knitting, crocheting, weaving) to local refugee women with the hope that it will bring "healing and creativity to their lives."

Months later Jennifer reflected on her moment with Belinda:

That day last fall, when I was talking with you, and your very nice
husband came up to us and spoke those few, very kind . . . words to
me, it really took me by surprise. I've never considered myself as being

beautiful. I don't think I'm ugly by any means, but neither do I think I'm beautiful. I've only ever been told that I have pretty eyes because my eyelashes are long and fairly thick. To hear that a grown man, one who doesn't even know me or my story, thinks that I have a beautiful face is truly an incredible moment. I was quite humbled and in awe. It was such a tender moment for me that the tears just flowed. To someone whose body is marred by burns and a bit deformed because of those unsightly scars, the words "You have a beautiful face" offer buckets and buckets full of hope . . . a reminder that I am a new creation in Christ.[21]

Every once in a while, God lets us peer into a life of inconceivable suffering, marked with such compelling faith and staggering hope that we cannot look away. Hope like this can catapult fledgling faith, galvanize even the shakiest of hearts, and help us believe that if God cares enough to impart breathtaking hope to a four-year-old girl struggling for life, then he cares about *all* suffering, *all* people, and their healing too.

Remaking the world requires people like you and me to forge faith in different fires so we can find within ourselves the courage to reach beyond our border fences, to believe differently, to hope powerfully, and to live out these values in ways that include the forgotten, considering them as future leaders, even heroes. "Christianity," says Moltmann, "is completely and entirely and utterly hope—a looking forward and a forward direction; hope is not just an appendix."[22]

Everything starts and ends with hope.

a word after: all things

Those who dream by night, in the dusty
recesses of their minds, wake in the day to
find that it was vanity: but the dreamers of
the day are dangerous . . . , for they may
act on their dreams with open eyes, to
make them possible.

—T. E. Lawrence

You may be well on your way toward living out a vision of change in
your community. Or maybe you don't know what the next thing is, but
you know you cannot ignore it any longer. Maybe that means just being willing to let God interrupt your life. If you don't know, simply "go where your
best prayers take you"[1] and, most of all, act on those prayers.

When you do, you will be surprised.

But it won't be easy. When it comes to doing good in a world with so
much talk and so little action, we owe God and the world both diligence and
perseverance. Jesus calls you and me to do extraordinary things, but we know
Jesus didn't preach a comfortable message. After a stunning statement about
wealth, salvation, a needle, and a camel, Jesus left his followers in a quandary

about the possibility of salvation: "Who then can be saved?" asked his follow-ers. But Jesus answered by saying, "With God all things are possible."[2] "Where humanity is helpless," says R. T. France, "God can."[3]

If only God would work unilaterally, without us, then he would surely get more done and much faster. When it comes to a changed heart, we depend upon God. But don't we depend on him for a changed world too? It remains a profound mystery why he chooses to work with and through us to bring the full range of his salvation to the world. But he asks us to join him, and so we must quit apologizing, gather our courage, dream dangerously, and live radical lives.

During the final edit of this book, I received a note through a colleague from Honorine, a woman in East Africa who took hold of some of the ideas in this book with rare pursuit. She told us how she chose not to respond to an insult, saying she wanted "to live in peace with her neighbor" instead. She talked about wanting her "beliefs to bear good fruit." She said everyone "was amazed because they all expected [her] to intervene" with hatred, bitterness, or even revenge against her neighbor.[4] She chose love instead. The Spirit of God, the community of faith, and a few ideas about a tree helped her make that choice.

Maybe her neighbors will follow suit.

Just one meaningful story by one person courageous enough to live her life differently in one of the most conflict-ridden areas of the world.

A radical life.

I like to dream about the mass of people across the world who profess faith in Jesus Christ. What if two billion people were to take a risk like Hono-rine? Is this just a fanciful pipe dream? I don't think so. Would the world change? I think we'd be stunned how fast.

As this book goes to print, the wounds of the world are not abating, and suffering is on the rise. Where your joy intersects with the world's pain is where you will bring hope to a weary world. It's also where you will personally thrive.

As we contemplate a better world tomorrow, we have the rare luxury to "dwell in possibility"[5] as never before in history. Give yourself permission to dream. Cast your fear to the wind. Follow the One who asks you to join him, who says, "All things are possible." You owe it to God, yourself, and the people who will thank you one day. And as you do, you will become a billboard for changing how we change the world.

The God of the universe will not, *cannot,* fully rest as long as one girl is lost to slavery, one mother cannot feed her family, or one boy is forced to pick up an AK-47. And we cannot fully rest either, because we are Christ here on earth—his hands reaching out, his feet pressing on, his blood coursing through our veins, his voice shouting when others won't speak up, his words triumphant until "injustice shuts its mouth" once and for all.[6]

Compassion, according to Frederick Buechner, is "knowing that there can never really be any peace and joy for any until there is peace and joy finally for all."[7] We are called to give our lives, fully and entirely, no matter the cost or prognosis. Jesus gave his life for us and, in so doing, converted our fickle hearts into flaming fire and exchanged all things impossible for that which can be.

One of the most impacting moments for me while writing this book was meeting Charlene, the woman I introduced in chapter 9. I don't think I've met a human being who has suffered more—her husband dead, her children hungry, and her body abused so many times. Yet she is one of the most joyful people I've ever met. Her faith towers above mine.

On the plane home I pondered a question: What if Charlene were I, and I were she? If so, when she returned home, would she forget Belinda and me? Or would she move heaven and earth to overcome our suffering and the suffering of those around us?

I think she would do *all* she could, because through her suffering God has remade her into a world changer. I think she would find a megaphone or two. And she would recruit others—hundreds, maybe thousands—to pick up their megaphones too, whether through pen or brush, spreadsheet or spoken word, story or song.

Of course, in a very real way, she and we are already *one*. Because we belong to each other, we experience a shared story. And together we can put the world right again.

Because with God, all things are possible.

APPENDIX A

the beautiful tree

a tool for discovering and designing change

This tool will help you lead a practical process toward change in a neighborhood, village, church, organization, club, or group. It empowers those involved to discover and play a role in bringing change to their community. It can also be used to diagnose change at the individual and personal level, but this tool is best used in a group setting. It is especially helpful in diagnosing broken relationships—whether between individuals or groups, both within and outside the community—and understanding what can be done to restore them. This tool can be applied at the beginning of a project, partnership, or plan; during an assessment or review; or even when things are not working out so well.

The ideas presented here are based on a biblical theory of change that aligns and integrates beliefs, values, and behaviors based on the text we looked at earlier:[1]

No good tree bears bad fruit, nor does a bad tree bear good fruit. . . . Good people bring good things out of the good stored up in their heart, and evil people bring evil things out of the evil stored up in their heart.[2]

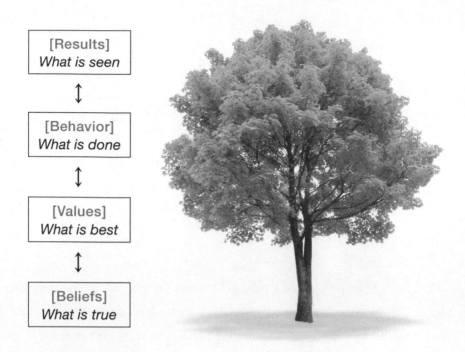

Sustainable change occurs when beliefs, values, and behaviors align within a biblical model of change.[3] Key ideas related to such a model include the following:

- When Jesus used the word *heart,* he meant the center of human life, the whole person, which includes the intellect, emotions, and will.
- In the model that follows, *beliefs* and *values* together constitute the heart, the center of human life.
- *Beliefs* are what we consider to be true. They are not just intellectual but emotional as well. How we think and what we feel make up our beliefs.[4]
- *Values* are what we prioritize as most important. We act or choose based on our values.
- *Behavior* is what we do as a result of choices informed by our values.

Let's explore how the model works in these phases: *what is* and then *what could be.*

Understand what is.

Within a group, or with a leader or friend, use the tree to understand the problem, or problems, by simply asking, *what is?* Depending on your context, you may want to have someone draw a picture of a tree or refer to a nearby tree. Begin with the top of the tree and move downward, listing the group's answers as you go and connecting, with arrows, the *Results, Behaviors, Values,* and *Beliefs.*

- What fruit do you see? Is it good fruit? bad fruit?
- What behaviors are producing the good or bad fruit?
- What values are leading to the behaviors that produce good or bad fruit?
- What beliefs are informing the values that lead to the behaviors?

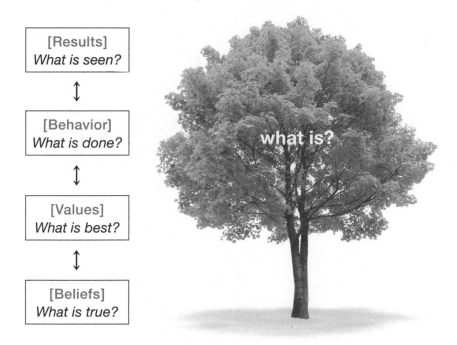

[Results]
What is seen?

↕

[Behavior]
What is done?

↕

[Values]
What is best?

↕

[Beliefs]
What is true?

what is?

Envision what could be.

Now, focusing on the bad fruit at the top of the tree, ask what the group desires instead. As you do, you may want to circle or highlight the good fruit in one color and the bad fruit in another, along with the corresponding behaviors, values, and beliefs. List the desired fruit next to the bad in a different color. Now move down the tree, listing the corresponding behaviors, values, and beliefs for the desired fruit as you consider these questions:

- What fruit do we desire?
- What behaviors would produce this fruit?
- What values would produce the behaviors we desire?
- What beliefs would inform the values that lead to the behaviors and results we desire?

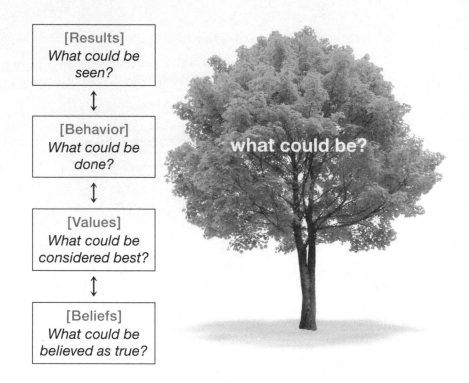

[Results]
What could be seen?

↕

[Behavior]
What could be done?

↕

[Values]
What could be considered best?

↕

[Beliefs]
What could be believed as true?

what could be?

Now that you've facilitated a vision of what could be, compare it to what should be:

- Does the fruit we desire reflect the nature and character of God's will?
- Are the behaviors we desire Christlike?
- Are the values we desire God centered?
- Are the beliefs we desire biblical?

Your group should now have a pretty good idea of the problems in its community, along with any gaps along the tree—those disconnects between what the community believes and values and how it behaves. You should also have some thoughts about how one or more of the problems could be overcome with a better set of beliefs, values, and behaviors.

In a very real sense, you have accomplished two important things: (a) an understanding of the issues and (b) a vision for the future. And perhaps most important, you've achieved this *with* the community, not *for* it. In fact, the community members have done the work themselves, and that makes all the difference.

Appendix B builds upon this tool by helping you mobilize, implement, and multiply change.

APPENDIX B

mapping a better future

a tool for mobilizing, implementing, and multiplying change

When done well, the art of releasing and multiplying assets within a community—whether talents, capabilities, or resources—can be nothing short of breathtaking.

But before we begin, let's first clarify what we mean by "community" and "assets."

A community is defined by something that is *shared* or held in common. What is shared can range from the conceptual (goals, values, beliefs, or a complaint) to the practical (location, profession, a business, an artist or interest group, and everything in between). Your community may be a small group, a classroom, a university club, a local church, a village leadership council, a neighborhood committee, a business, a nonprofit, or just a collection of friends who want to make a difference. Your props may be hands-on (from a flip chart with Post-its to a sand pit with a stick to draw with) or virtual (Google Docs, Facebook, or advanced project software). Whatever your context, the principles of asset mapping cut across all.

Assets contain inherent and/or conferred value. They are "useful and desirable things."[1] Relationships between assets—social or spiritual capital—can also become assets themselves. Once community members discover what is valuable among them, they are empowered to care, and once they discover what they care about, they can take action. Action, in turn, inspires more change.

Remember, through the process of mapping, hope emerges, and the impossible becomes possible.

Focusing on strengths, or assets, is a different way to see the world. What if the proverbial glass is neither half-full nor half-empty? What if both halves are opportunities—what is possible instead of only problematic? Perhaps you already began to experience this shift during the tree exercise.

Understanding how change happens in our own hearts as well as within local and global communities is a prerequisite for sustaining and multiplying change. We can avoid superficial, short-lived solutions by learning what must change at a root level.

You may have realized by now that the tree tool both diagnoses and appreciates; it speaks to reality but also dreams. It should have led you through a process of defining and discovering *what is* and, by dreaming and envisioning, *what could be* and even *what should be*. In essence you completed a diagnostic process to understand what needed to change, and then you facilitated an appreciative process to dream about a better way.

Now you can bring these dreams into reality by inspiring action.

Asset mapping creates a trajectory of hope, a better tomorrow, by building a plan, program, or project in the context of relationships—your community. Mapping matches the assets to action, both internal and external, including between specific spheres of influence. The steps involved are flexible and can be applied within any community, whether a group, a home, a family, a church, a neighborhood, a collection of artists or athletes, a for-profit or nonprofit, whether on-site or virtual, local or global.

Mapping considers three pivotal actors:

- *People*. Human capital is foundational for all strength-based change. Identifying, mobilizing, and engaging the gifts, abilities, and skills of all people—including children, youth, and the elderly—are vital within any context.
- *Groups*. Social capital, the strength generated through relationships and networks, is essential in any situation needing change. Prayer groups, youth groups, trade guilds or associations, clubs, sports teams, and study groups should all be considered.
- *Organizations*. The purpose and culture of an organization, whether businesses, hospitals, churches, schools, nonprofits, or parks, have tremendous potential to affect a community positively.

Together, these three groups represent the community, and many communities together represent society. Using tools to assess, or inventory, the capacities of people, groups, and an organization is a fascinating exercise. Invariably people discover strengths they didn't know existed. The results almost always surprise.

Let's begin.

Step 1: Build a team.

Asset mapping is best done in community. To that end, your role as a facilitator is essential. Remember, your community may be a small group, a classroom, a local church, a village leadership council, a neighborhood committee, or a collection of friends. Your members could come from

- key places of influence and leadership,
- key places of opinion and understanding, or
- key places of faith and spiritual strength.

Who leads this process makes all the difference because that person paves the way for effective and creative change. Take your time; invest in your process for selecting a team. Consider looking for the following principles and attitudes:

- *Members should be ready to place strengths first.* They should see a community, an issue, or an individual first as an asset rather than a deficit, focusing on what is possible in light of a community's strengths while not ignoring its problems.
- *Members should value a shared agenda.* They should be willing to share knowledge and opinions and to set goals and action steps from a position of mutuality. Remember, participation creates ownership, and cooperation enables action.
- *Members should be relationship driven.* They should be willing to co-learn, cooperate, consult, and co-create by placing people at the heart of the solution. The best facilitators *respond* to people rather than *direct* people.

Helping your team birth ideas and eventually convert them into viable actions is an essential function, and a learned skill, for a facilitator. It's also important to set your success metrics well. When the people within a community begin setting their own agendas, establishing their own goals, and acting on their plans without outside initiation, you are succeeding. These are the indicators of future heroes!

Mapping sessions can be conducted literally anywhere, from boardrooms with smart boards to rural villages with sand and stones. I have seen community maps created with crayons, markers, sticks, scraps of newspaper, index cards, LEGOs, and various flora and vegetation. What your team uses to represent its various assets is as limitless as your cumulative creativity and available resources.

Your team should reflect the composition in your community. If you are working with a church, your asset-mapping team should reflect a wide variety of members—age, gender, and race—found within the church. If you are working with a rural village, your team should include representatives from all ethnicities. Diversity creates synergy within teams and brings a beautiful richness and truer perspective to an asset map.[2]

Step 2: Define your community.

Now that you've built a team, bring the members together and ask:

- What is your first thought when you think of this community?
- How would you define this community? By name? By geography? By interest? By culture? By religious affiliation? By economic standards? A combination of all of these?

Remember it is easier to build a solution from the glass half-full (assets) than half-empty (deficits), so focus your team on defining the community from *what it is* rather than *what it is not*. If you led your team through the tree exercise, you should already have an idea of *what is, what could be,* and even *what should be.* Now you can begin to map assets toward achieving that change.

You may want to consider what statement, or symbol, defines your community. Decide on one as a group, and place it at the center of the space you are working in. You might, for example, define your community as a neighborhood in Portland focused on ending trafficking, a university interested in engaging the immigration issue, a virtual community advocating against the conflict in the Central African Republic, or a business inviting its employees to engage in charity.

Step 3: Discover your assets.

Now ask your team to spend time reflecting on the people, groups, and organizations connected to your community, naming the assets found in each.

Discuss and write them down. You may choose to write them on Post-its or index cards, for example. Then place the Post-its in radiating groups around your community definition or symbol as shown below. Some assets may belong to more than one group, and some assets may not fit perfectly in any group. Anomalies happen; best guesses and multiple answers are perfectly acceptable.

The central question is this: What assets will help you achieve the change you defined in the tree exercise? Consider the three areas we discussed earlier as you reflect together:

- *People.* What are the community's valuable gifts, abilities, skills, and relationships, and to whom do they belong?
- *Groups.* What are the community's valuable *collections* of people? These can be as wide-ranging as social, spiritual, institutional, economic, special interest, and so on. Sometimes

there are groups within groups that can be considered, such as youth groups, trade guilds, artist cooperatives, study groups— all representing community assets.

- *Organizations.* What are the community's valuable structured groups with collective goals? Consider businesses, religions, government offices, nonprofits, educational institutions, media outlets, parks and museums, local schools, and so on. Occasionally it is helpful to recognize the separate parts that make up an organization as individual assets.

Step 4: Bridge your assets.

Often the greatest strengths in a mapping exercise emerge when connecting one asset to another. Certain bridges, or connections, can help the community realize its better future and restore broken relationships. As your team reflects on its people, groups, and organizations, think through these questions:

- *What natural bridges exist <u>within</u> each of the three groups you created?* Does the mayor know your pastor? Does your study group know the artist guild? Does the restaurant know the school? What is the nature of the bridges between each of them? Formal or informal? Close or distant? Welcoming or hostile? Tackle each group separately, moving your Post-its into pairs or small groups of logical and creative connections, or you might draw lines connecting one to another.
- *What bridges exist <u>between</u> each of the groups you are creating?* Do your mayor and your pastor know of the artist group that advocates for clean water? Does the restaurant that hosts your Bible study care about hunger in the homeless groups around town? Create bridges by moving your pairs and groups together with other groups as shown on the next page.

Remember, community asset mapping is dynamic and open-ended. Synergy will build as ideas flow. A person may spark an idea about a group that triggers an idea of an organization that leads to another key influencer, and so on. Sometimes sessions that seem the most chaotic produce the most vibrant and helpful maps. So organize your map as your team sees best with the goal of change. Remember your role as facilitator and initiator: be selective when offering advice or suggestions. You role is to cooperate with the process and move it forward.

Step 5: Take action.

In order for a community to move forward toward change, its assets must be released, or activated. Giving action to community assets, including especially the relationships that can bring life, even justice, is one of the most exciting steps in creating change.

Begin by asking two questions:
- What *can* we do?
- What *should* we do?

As you and your team review the bridges between your community assets, list and prioritize your most promising connections, or bridges, and give action to them. What action words seem to fit naturally with these bridges? Consider the following list to help stimulate your thinking toward putting feet to your vision. Remember your commitment to prioritizing strengths, sharing agendas, and remaining relationally oriented as you move into the decision-making phase.

campaign	auction	exhibition	meeting
program	survey	performance	event
project	celebration	blog	tweet
scholarship	kickstart	petition	conference
award	editorial	gala	open-mic
prayer	research	vigil	race
study	symposium	concert	letter

As you consider what you will do, write out what asset-based actions your team recommends. What is the end goal of this project? How will you know the project has succeeded? Let your asset map help you create lists of actions to move your project forward. As you do, ask a member of the group to take the lead on each action step. Add a date next to each if possible. Remember, the bridges between groups will spark ideas for resources and relationships to help you make progress toward your goals. Make sure your final action step is to evaluate how successfully the project is accomplishing its goals throughout the process. Community participation in both the execution and evaluation of your actions is absolutely vital to fostering change.

Well done! You have begun to implement sustainable change, through others, from the bottom up.

notes

chapter 1: do we dare disturb the universe?

1. Joseph Conrad, "Geography and Some Explorers" (1924), *Last Essays,* ed. Harold Ray Stevens and J. H. Stape (Cambridge: Cambridge University Press, 2011), 14.
2. For more information on joining the Wage Peace community, see www.worldrelief.org/wagepeace.
3. C. S. Lewis, *Weight of Glory* (1942; repr., New York: HarperCollins, 2009), 146.
4. Gordon Conway and Katy Wilson, *One Billion Hungry: Can We Feed the World?* www.canwefeedtheworld.org/; Didi Kirsten Tatlow, "27 Million People Said to Live in 'Modern Slavery,'" *New York Times,* June 20, 2013, http://rendezvous.blogs.nytimes.com/2013/06/20/27-million-people-said-to-live-in-modern-slavery/?_php=true&_type=blogs&_r=0.
5. By "majority world" I am referring to the non-Western world, avoiding less-honoring descriptors such as "the developing world" or "Third World."
6. T. S. Eliot, "The Love Song of J. Alfred Prufrock," in *Collected Poems, 1909–1962* (New York: Harcourt Brace Jovanovich, 1991), 4.
7. Dallas Willard, *The Spirit of the Disciplines: Understanding How God Changes Lives* (New York: HarperCollins, 1988), xii.

8. Quoted in Laura Turner, "And Like It Began It Ends: Bill Hybels on the Local Church," Loturner.com, August 10, 2012, Loturner.com, http://loturner.com/and-like-it-began-it-ends-bill-hybels-on-the -local-church/.

9. Micah 6:8, NASB.

10. Tim Keller, *The Difference Between an Adventure and a Quest,* March 10, 2014, Cassiciacum, http://cassiciacum.wordpress.com/2014/03/10 /tim-keller-on-the-difference-between-an-adventure-and-a-quest/.

11. *The Lord of the Rings: The Fellowship of the Ring,* directed by Peter Jackson (Los Angeles: New Line Cinema, 2001).

12. John Greenleaf Whittier, "My Soul and I," 1847, www.readbookonline .net/readOnLine/7960/.

13. Kurt Schork, "Kurt Schork's signature dispatch from Sarajevo," Reuters, May 23, 1993, www.ksmemorial.com/romeo.htm.

14. Robert Frost, *The Poetry of Robert Frost* (New York: Henry Holt, 1969), 105.

15. One journalist referred to Mandela's "superhuman forgiveness" as a "holy magnanimity." See Tom Lodge, *Politics in South Africa: From Mandela to Mbeki,* 2nd ed. (Indianapolis: Indiana University Press, 2003), 14.

16. Desmond Tutu and Nelson Mandela are often credited as seminal figures who, among others, helped spare their country from an outburst of violence following the apartheid era. From Michael Jesse Battle, *Reconciliation: The Ubuntu Theology of Desmond Tutu,* rev. ed. (Cleveland: Pilgrim Press, 2009), 1.

17. Nelson Mandela in a 2005 speech before twenty-two thousand people in Trafalgar Square in London, emphasis added. BBC, February 3, 2005, http://news.bbc.co.uk/2/hi/uk_news/politics/4232603.stm. By generation, I don't mean to imply age. The invitation in this book is

psychographic rather than *demographic*. It's about "an attitude, not an age bracket," says Steve Moore in *Genflux: Why a Nextgen Friendly Culture Is What Your Organization Needs and Everybody Wants,* Missio Nexus, 3. www.missionexus.org/genflux-why-a-nextgen-friendly -culture-is-what-your-organization-needs-and-everybody-wants/.

chapter 2: the fierce urgency of now

1. Diarmaid MacCulloch, *Christianity: The First Three Thousand Years* (London: Penguin, 2011), 577.

2. Romans 1:17, NKJV.

3. In his book *The Triumph of Christianity: How the Jesus Movement Became the World's Largest Religion* (New York: HarperCollins, 2011), Rodney Stark makes a strong case for an urban, bourgeoisie reformation instead of the traditionally held rural, peasant reformation. Only 3–5 percent of Germany was literate in 1500, so the fire of the Reformation spread among the educated class—professors, students, merchants, and nobles. But the promise of the Reformation remains true: *anyone can access God by faith alone.* The peasantry was significantly helped by the radical shifts of the Reformation. The injustice of indulgences ceased, but their long-term effects took root over time. All said, going viral in the sixteenth century took time, even with Gutenberg's press.

4. "Every Child Deserves a 5th Birthday," USAID, 2014, http://5thbday .usaid.gov/pages/Home.aspx.

5. Martin Luther King Jr., "Beyond Vietnam: A Time to Break Silence: Declaration of Independence from the War in Vietnam" (speech, Riverside Church in New York City, April 4, 1967), http://mlk-kpp01 .stanford.edu/index.php/encyclopedia/documentsentry/doc_beyond _vietnam/.

6. Rick Warren, Beliefnet, www.beliefnet.com/Faiths/Christianity/2005/10/Rick-Warrens-Second-Reformation.aspx.

7. The word *reform* comes from the Latin *reformare,* meaning "to form again, to shape, change or alter." In the early fifteenth century, *reform* meant "to bring a person, people, or institution from an evil course of life," and by the 1700s it meant to amend what is wrong. *Reformation* is distinguished from *revolution,* the former seeking to correct serious wrongs without altering the whole, the latter seeking wholesale, radical change. "The Reformation" refers to the Protestant Reformation of the sixteenth century and often also the Counter, or Catholic, Reformation that followed. But there have been many reformers and reformations throughout history, from the early Monastics to Patrick and the Celts, to Dominic and Francis of Assisi, to the Anabaptists, the Puritans, and Moravians, to the Methodists of the eighteenth century and beyond.

8. Brennan Manning, *The Ragamuffin Gospel: Good News for the Bedraggled, Beat-Up, and Burnt Out* (New York: Doubleday Religious Publishing Group, 2008), Kindle edition, location 610.

9. MacCulloch, *Christianity,* 338–40. Thousands are still lured to the pilgrimage across the Pyrenees to Compostela, the renowned site in Spain. Modern-day pilgrims recount the journey as transformational, life changing, and awakening. Actor Martin Sheen made a movie about Compostela called *The Way.*

10. Kenneth S. Latourette, *A History of Christianity* (Peabody, MA: Prince Press, 1999), 701.

11. Joan D. Hedrick, *Harriet Beecher Stowe: A Life* (New York: Oxford University Press, 1995), 208.

12. David B. Sachsman, S. Kittrell Rushing, and Roy Morris Jr., eds., *Memory and Myth: The Civil War in Fiction and Film from Uncle*

Tom's Cabin to Cold Mountain (West Lafayette, IN: Purdue University Press, 2007), 8.

13. 2 Corinthians 12:9; 1 Corinthians 1:27–28.

14. Taken from a 2010 interview with World Relief staff members who facilitate the Way of Hope cell church movement in Cambodia.

15. In his biography of Desmond Tutu, John Allen refers to "regular occurrences in which [Tutu] often stood between two groups . . . carrying bricks and stones." While this specific instance is attributed to Tutu, it seems to be undocumented. John Allen, *Rabble-Rouser for Peace: The Authorized Biography of Desmond Tutu* (New York: Free Press, 2006), Kindle edition.

16. Stephan Bauman, "Laugh When Devils Cry," 2013.

17. Jonathan Martin, Twitter post, September 7, 2013, @theboyonthebike.

18. Dietrich Bonhoeffer, *The Cost of Discipleship* (New York: Simon and Schuster, 1995), 47.

19. Martin Luther King Jr., "I've Been to the Mountaintop," *American Rhetoric,* April 3, 1968, www.americanrhetoric.com/speeches/mlk ivebeentothemountaintop.htm.

20. James Davison Hunter, "Faithful Presence," interview by Christopher Benson, *Christianity Today* 54, no. 5 (May 2010): 33.

21. See Psalm 62:8.

22. Paul Brandeis Raushenbush, "50 Years Later: Whither the Moral Arc of the Universe?" *Huffington Post,* August 23, 2013, www .huffingtonpost.com/paul-raushenbush/march-on-washington -anniversary_b_3786410.html.

chapter 3: there's more to you than you know

1. C. S. Lewis, *Surprised by Joy: The Shape of My Early Life* (New York: Houghton Mifflin, 1966), 230.

2. Alister McGrath, *C. S. Lewis: A Life* (Carol Stream, IL: Tyndale, 2012), 137.

3. McGrath, *C. S. Lewis,* 149, 152.

4. Alister McGrath, *The Intellectual World of C. S. Lewis* (Malden, MA: John Wiley & Sons, 2014), 105.

5. J. R. R. Tolkien, *The Hobbit* (New York: Houghton Mifflin, 2014), 104.

6. Psalm 37:4, NASB.

7. Ephesians 2:10, NLT and NIV.

8. John 15:16.

9. William Shakespeare, *King Lear* (Mineola, NY: Dover Publications, 2010), 1.4.10.

10. Quoted from a 2013 conversation with Tim Amstutz, country leader for World Relief Cambodia.

11. Ellen and Benevento Langer, "Self-Induced Dependence," *Journal of Personality and Social Psychology* 36, no. 8 (August 1978): 886.

12. See John 15:16.

13. Mother Teresa, quoted in Malcolm Muggeridge, *Something Beautiful for God* (San Francisco: Harper One, 2003), 15.

14. John 17:20.

15. John 14:12–14, NIV 2011, emphasis added.

16. Os Guinness, *The Call: Finding and Fulfilling the Central Purpose of Your Life* (Nashville: W Publishing, 2003), 31, 39.

17. Martin Luther, "The Estate of Marriage" (1522), http://pages.uoregon.edu/dluebke/Reformations441/LutherMarriage.htm.

18. Tim Keller, "Vocation: Discerning Your Calling," www.coindy.org/wp-content/uploads/Vocation-DiscerningYourCalling.pdf.

19. See 1 Peter 2:9.

20. See Isaiah 61:1–2.

21. Roko Belic, *Happy* (New York: Wadi Rum Films, 2012).

22. See 2 Corinthians 5:20.

23. Jürgen Moltmann, *The Church in the Power of the Spirit: A Contribu-tion to Messianic Ecclesiology,* trans. Margaret Kohl (Minneapolis: Fortress, 1993), 73.

24. C. S. Lewis, *Mere Christianity* (New York: Harper One, 2001), 177.

25. "Catechism of the Catholic Church," CatholicCulture.org, emphasis added, www.catholicculture.org/culture/library/catechism/index.cfm ?recnum=3008.

26. John 15:5, 7.

27. N. T. Wright, *Surprised by Hope* (San Francisco: HarperCollins, 2012), 200, 207, emphasis added.

28. William Wrede, *Paul,* trans. Edward Lummis (London: Philip Green, 1907), 100.

29. See Tyler Wigg-Stevenson, *The World Is Not Ours to Save: Finding the Freedom to Do Good* (Downers Grove, IL: InterVarsity, 2013), where he cautions against putting ourselves in the place of God.

30. Wright, *Surprised by Hope,* 207.

31. Quoted in John Ortberg, "Dallas Willard, a Man from Another 'Time Zone,'" *Christianity Today,* May 8, 2013, www.ctlibrary.com/ct/2013 /may-web-only/man-from-another-time-zone.html.

32. Philippians 4:13.

33. Isaiah 43:1–2.

34. Gary Haugen (talk, Elmbrook Church, Brookfield, WI, October 2012).

chapter 4: awakening your life

1. Isaiah 42:9.

2. Henry David Thoreau, *Walden and On the Duty of Civil Disobedi-ence,* www.gutenberg.org/files/205/205-h/205-h.htm.

3. Joseph Campbell, *The Hero with a Thousand Faces* (Novato, CA: New World Library, 2008), 29–30.

4. Elizabeth Barrett Browning, "Aurora Leigh," *Aurora Leigh and Other Poems* (New York: Penguin, 2006), 232.

5. Frederick Buechner, *Listening to Your Life* (San Francisco: HarperSanFrancisco, 1992), 2.

6. Bill Hybels, Twitter post, March 9, 2014, https://twitter.com/wcagls /status/442744129441628160.

7. Buechner, *Listening,* 186.

8. Dante Alighieri, *The Divine Comedy of Dante Alighieri,* trans. James Romanes Sibbald, Inferno Canto 1:1–60.

9. C. S. Lewis, *Of Other Worlds: Essays and Stories* (San Diego: Harvest Books, 2002).

10. John 15:2, NKJV.

11. Florence Scovel Shinn, *The Complete Works of Florence Scovel Shinn* (New York: Dover Publications, 2010), 13.

12. Philippians 3:12.

13. William Wrede, *Paul,* trans. Edward Lummis (London: Philip Green, 1907), 100, quoted in Michael Gorman, *Becoming the Gospel: Paul, Participation, and Mission* (Eugene, OR: Wipf and Stock, 2015).

14. John 15:16, NIV 2011.

15. Wynton Marsalis in "Gumbo," *Jazz: A Film by Ken Burns,* episode 1 (Walpole, NH: Florentine Films, PBS, 2001).

16. Charles Duhigg, *The Power of Habit: Why We Do What We Do in Life and Business* (New York: Random House, 2012), 131, 47.

17. Patrick Henry, ed., *Benedict's Dharma: Buddhists Reflect on the Rule of Saint Benedict* (New York: Riverhead Books, 2002), 1.

18. See Stephen Macchia, *Crafting a Rule of Life: An Invitation to the Well-Ordered Way* (Downers Grove, IL: InterVarsity, 2012).

19. Based on the Greek equivalent, *homologeo*; see Spiros Zodhiates, *The Complete Word Study New Testament* (Chattanooga: AMG Publishers, 1991).

20. G. K. Chesterton, *The Collected Works of G. K. Chesterton*, vol. 1, *Heretics, Orthodoxy, the Blatchford Controversies* (San Francisco: Ignatius, 1986), 409.

chapter 5: six impossibilities before breakfast

1. Lewis Carroll, *Alice's Adventures in Wonderland,* 1865, www.alice -in-wonderland.net/books/2chpt5.html.

2. Interview, *USA Today,* February 24, 2012.

3. William Belsham, *Memoirs of the Reign of George III from His Accession, to the Peace of Amiens,* vol. 4 (1805; repr., Charleston, SC: Nabu Press, 2011), 439.

4. Iphigenia Mukataban, quoted in Christine Amanpour, "Woman Opens Heart to Man Who Slaughtered Her Family," CNN, May 15, 2008, www.cnn.com/2008/WORLD/africa/05/15 /amanpour.rwanda/.

5. Matthew 3:8, NASB.

6. Matthew 25:37–40, NIV 2011.

7. Dallas Willard, *The Divine Conspiracy: Rediscovering Our Hidden Life in God* (San Francisco: HarperSanFrancisco, 1988), 25.

8. Matthew 6:10.

9. Matthew 5:43–44, NIV 2011.

10. James 2:17.

11. United States Declaration of Independence, 1776, https://history .state.gov/milestones/1776-1783/declaration.

12. Article 1 of the United Nations Universal Declaration of Human Rights, 1948, www.un.org/en/documents/udhr/.

13. See Genesis 50:20, where Joseph concludes that God used the evil plot against him by his brothers for good.

14. Quoted in John Ortberg, *Who Is This Man? The Unpredictable Impact of the Inescapable Jesus* (Grand Rapids: Zondervan, 2012), n.p.

15. International Federation of Red Cross, "Horn of Africa: A Letter from Turkana, Northern Kenya," July 26, 2011, www.ifrc.org/en/news -and-media/opinions-and-positions/opinion-pieces/2011/horn-of -africa--a-letter-from-turkana-northern-kenya/.

16. Louis Berkhof, *Systematic Theology,* 4th ed. (Grand Rapids: Eerdmans, 1979), 434–35.

17. Quoted in Malcolm Muggeridge, "The Humane Holocaust," *Human Life Review* (Winter 1980), emphasis added.

18. U.S. State Department, *International Religious Freedom Report 2003,* Bureau of Democracy, Human Rights and Labor, www.state.gov/j/drl /rls/irf/2003/23746.htm.

19. Matthew 7:23, NKJV.

20. Bryant Myers, *Walking with the Poor: Principles and Practices of Transformational Development* (Maryknoll, NY: Orbis, 1999), 78.

21. E. Stanley Jones, *The Unchanging Person and the Unshakable Kingdom* (Nashville: Abingdon, 1972), 30.

22. Walter Wink, *Engaging the Powers: Discernment and Resistance in a World of Domination* (Minneapolis: Fortress, 1992), 83.

23. Matthew 6:10.

24. See Jesus's mandate in Luke 4:18–19 and Isaiah 61:1–2: "The Spirit of the Lord is on me, because he has anointed me to preach good news to the poor. He has sent me to proclaim freedom for the prisoners and recovery of sight for the blind, to release the oppressed, to proclaim the year of the Lord's favor."

25. See 2 Corinthians 5:18; Romans 8:19–21.

26. Nicholas Wolterstorff, *Justice: Rights and Wrongs* (Princeton, NJ: Princeton University Press, 2008), 55.

27. See Isaiah 1:16 and Alec J. Motyer, *The Prophecy of Isaiah: An Introduction and Commentary* (Downers Grove, IL: InterVarsity, 1993), 47.

28. Deuteronomy 6:5.

29. Matthew 22:39.

30. Timothy Keller, *Generous Justice: How God's Grace Makes Us Just* (London: Penguin Books, 2010), 10.

31. Quoted in Duncan Forrester, *Christian Justice and Public Policy* (Cambridge: Cambridge University Press, 1997), 55.

chapter 6: when caterpillars fly

1. Based on a conversation with Bethany Anderson from Solidarity, in Pasadena, CA, 2012.

2. *Encyclopedia Britannica Online,* s.v. "Cogito, Ergo Sum," www.britannica.com/EBchecked/topic/124443/cogito-ergo-sum.

3. James K. A. Smith, *Desiring the Kingdom: Worship, Worldview, and Cultural Formation* (Grand Rapids: Baker Academic, 2009), 75.

4. Will Durant, *The Story of Philosophy: The Lives and Opinions of the World's Greatest Philosophers* (1926; repr., New York: Simon & Schuster, 1991), 76.

5. Luke 6:43–44.

6. Luke 6:45, TNIV.

7. As far as I can tell, Darrow Miller, in *Discipling Nations* (Seattle, WA: YWAM Publishing, 2001), first put forward a model that uses the concept of a tree to express the drivers of truth and lies. Some say the basic idea is sourced elsewhere, however. Whatever the origin, I am indebted to the essential idea, which I build upon here, leaning heavily upon Paul Hiebert, *Transforming Worldviews: An Anthropological*

Understanding of How People Change (Grand Rapids: Baker Academic, 2008).

8. Hiebert, *Transforming Worldviews,* 25–26.

9. Hiebert, *Transforming Worldviews,* 25.

10. Dallas Willard, *The Divine Conspiracy: Rediscovering Our Hidden Life in God* (San Francisco: HarperSanFrancisco, 1998), 211.

11. Brennan Manning, *The Relentless Tenderness of Jesus* (Grand Rapids: Revell, 2004), 17–18.

12. 1 Corinthians 2:16.

13. John 17:11.

chapter 7: a beautiful collision

1. David Crowder, "A Beautiful Collision" (Sparrow Records/Sixsteps Records, EMI Christian Music Group, 2005).

2. John 8:7.

3. John 8:11.

4. Victor Hugo, *Les Misérables* (London: Penguin Books, 1976), 110–15.

5. Peter Berger, *The Sacred Canopy: Elements of a Sociological Theory of Religion* (1967; repr., New York: Open Road, 2011), Kindle edition, location 51.

6. Dietrich Bonhoeffer, *The Cost of Discipleship* (New York: Simon and Schuster, 1995), 152–53.

7. Bonhoeffer, *Cost of Discipleship,* 153.

8. George Weigel, *Witness to Hope: The Biography of Pope John Paul II* (New York: HarperCollins, 2001), 293.

9. Peggy Noonan, "We Want God: When John Paul II Went to Poland, Communism Didn't Have a Prayer," *Wall Street Journal,* April 7, 2005, http://online.wsj.com/articles/SB1224794084584 63941.

10. Heather Saul, "Tiananmen Square: What Happened to Tank Man?" *Independent,* June 4, 2014, www.independent.co.uk/news/world/asia/tiananmen-square-what-happened-to-tank-man-9483398.html.

11. Steve and Marie Goode, directors of YWAM Mercy Ministries, vividly tell this story.

12. Luke 22:49–51; Luke 19:1–7; Matthew 26:6–13; Luke 23:34.

13. Andy Crouch, *Culture Making: Recovering Our Creative Calling* (Downers Grove, IL: InterVarsity, 2013), 191, 107.

14. James Davison Hunter, *To Change the World: The Irony, Tragedy, and Possibility of Christianity in the Late Modern World* (London: Oxford University Press, 2010), 14.

15. Norie Huddle, *Butterfly: A Tiny Tale of Great Transformation* (New York: Huddle Books, 1990), 6.

chapter 8: begin the world over again

1. "Iowa Rep. Tom Latham Pays Tribute to Dr. Borlaug," *The World Food Prize,* March 20, 2008, www.worldfoodprize.org/en/press/news/?action=display&newsID=8051.

2. Mark Stuertz, "Green Giant," *Dallas Observer,* December 5, 2002, www.dallasobserver.com/2002-12-05/news/green-giant/2/.

3. Gregg Easterbrook, "Forgotten Benefactor of Humanity," *The Atlantic,* January 1, 1997, www.theatlantic.com/magazine/archive/1997/01/forgotten-benefactor-of-humanity/306101/.

4. Norman Borlaug, Nobel Lecture, "The Green Revolution, Peace, and Humanity," December 11, 1970, www.nobelprize.org/nobel_prizes/peace/laureates/1970/borlaug-lecture.html.

5. Matthew 26:11.

6. Genesis 1:2.

7. Genesis 1:3, 26–27.

8. Genesis 1:31.

9. Genesis 1:28.

10. Albert M. Wolters, *Creation Regained: Biblical Basics for a Reformational Worldview* (Grand Rapids: Eerdmans, 2005), 41–42.

11. Genesis 2:15, emphasis added.

12. Nina Beth Cardin, "Seeking the Common Good" (lecture, St. Mary's Ecumenical Institute, Baltimore, MD, April 9, 2013).

13. Cardin, "Seeking the Common Good."

14. 2 Corinthians 5:17–20.

15. Wolters, *Creation Regained,* 44–45.

16. Dallas Willard, "Leadership and Spirituality" (lecture, Regent College, Vancouver, BC, May 15, 2000).

17. Henri J. M. Nouwen, *The Inner Voice of Love: A Journey Through Anguish to Freedom* (New York: Doubleday, 1998), 3.

18. Andy Crouch, *Playing God: Redeeming the Gift of Power* (Downers Grove, IL: InterVarsity, 2013), 17, 19.

19. George Herbert, "The Bag," *The Complete English Poems,* ed. John Tobin (New York: Penguin, 2005), 142.

20. Quoted in Kay Marshall Strom, *Once Blind: The Life of John Newton* (Colorado Springs: Authentic, 2008), 225.

21. Joel 2:28–29.

22. I am indebted to Jürgen Moltmann for describing the cross and resurrection as solidarity and protest. See *The Crucified God: The Cross of Christ as the Foundation and Criticism of Christian Theology,* trans. R. A. Wilson and John Bowden (Minneapolis: Fortress, 1993), 263.

23. See Matthew 6:10.

24. UNICEF, "Joint Report Details Escalating Global Orphan Crisis Due to AIDS," July 10, 2002, www.unicef.org/newsline/02pr43brink.htm.

25. Malcolm Gladwell refers to these people as "mavens," people with knowledge essential to the movement. See his book *The Tipping Point: How Little Things Can Make a Big Difference* (Boston: Little, Brown, and Company, 2000), 60.

26. Gladwell, *The Tipping Point,* 46.

27. Jenny Yang and Matthew Soerens, *Welcoming the Stranger* (Downers Grove, IL: InterVarsity, 2009). Over the last decade, Jenny and Matthew have informally influenced immigration legislation, including the US Senate bill that was passed in 2013.

28. Belinda Bauman, "Why Josh Garrels Is Giving Away His Music to Support Peace-Building in Congo," *Huffington Post,* March 26, 2013, www.huffingtonpost.com/belinda-bauman/interview-why-josh-garrel _b_2949635.html.

29. See Ephesians 4:11–13.

30. The word *passion* is derived from the Latin *passio,* which literally means "to suffer." See James Orr, *International Standard Bible Encyclopedia* (Peabody, MA: Hendrickson Publishers, 1915), www.biblestudytools .com/encyclopedias/isbe/passion-passions.html. Today *passion* is generally defined as emotional strength.

31. As you reflect upon your wisdom, you will likely identify areas of obvious overlap between your passion and wisdom; that is a good thing. They should inform one another. You will also find areas of wisdom you are not passionate about and areas of passion where you don't yet have much wisdom. You should expect that too. But you will also find areas of overlap that aren't so obvious; for example, experience in the arts could relate to a cause in ways you haven't considered, or hard skills like technology or design could translate exceptionally well across the world, even into small start-up situations.

32. You may choose to use mind map software or an app for this exercise. See, for example, the tools detailed at Lifehacker.com, http://lifehacker .com/five-best-mind-mapping-tools-476534555.

33. Young Jun Chan, "Proximity and Mind Map," Pennsylvania State University, March 18, 2014, http://sites.psu.edu/perceptionspring 14/2014/03/18/proximity-and-mind-map/; John W. Budd, "Mind Maps as Classroom Exercises," *Journal of Economic Education* 35, no. 1 (Winter 2004): 35–46, www.jstor.org/stable/30042572.

34. You can find more information at their website, www.strengthsfinder .com.

35. Daniel Pink, *Drive: The Surprising Truth About What Motivates Us* (New York: Riverhead, 2009), 79.

chapter 9: the making of heroes

1. Lynne Hybels, "I Paddled for Congo! #MaybeICan2013," *Lynnehybels* (blog), September 1, 2013, www.lynnehybels.com/i-paddled-for -congo-maybeican2013/.

2. Lynne Hybels, "Charlene's Story," *Lynnehybels* (blog), October 17, 2009, www.lynnehybels.com/charlenes-story.

3. Peter Ove, "'Change a Life. Change Your Own': Child Sponsorship, the Discourse of Development, and the Production of Ethical Subjects" (PhD diss., University of British Columbia, 2013), 7, http://circle.ubc .ca/handle/2429/44164.

4. Bruce Wydick, "Want to Change the World? Sponsor a Child," *Christianity Today,* June 14, 2013, www.christianitytoday.com/ct/2013 /june/want-to-change-world-sponsor-child.html.

5. Nicholas Kristof, "Where Is the Love?" *New York Times,* November 27, 2013, www.nytimes.com/2013/11/28/opinion/kristof-where-is -the-love.html?_r=0.

6. Ove, "Change," 251.

7. John Kretzmann and John McKnight, *Building Communities from the Inside Out* (Skokie, IL: ACTA Publications, 1993), 13.

8. Luke 3:8.

9. Luke 3:8, NLT.

10. Dictionary.com, s.v. "empathy," http://dictionary.reference.com /browse/empathy?s=t.

11. Santa Clara University, "Mother Teresa Reflects on Working Toward Peace," www.scu.edu/ethics/architects-of-peace/Teresa /essay.html.

12. Matthew 10:9–10, NLT.

chapter 10: hatching hope

1. See Luke 7:22.

2. See Matthew 5.

3. Luke 3:10–11, NIV 2011.

4. Luke 3:11, NLT.

5. Martin Luther, *The Table Talk or Familiar Discourse of Martin Luther,* trans. William Hazlitt (London: David Bogue, 1848), 146, emphasis added.

6. Spiros Zodhiates, ed. and comp., *The Complete Word Study New Testament: King James Version* (Chattanooga, TN: AMG Publishers, 1991), 1680.

7. Hebrews 11:1, NASB.

8. Colossians 1:27.

9. Luke 21:1–4.

10. 2 Kings 4:1–7.

11. Jürgen Moltmann, *Ethics of Hope,* trans. Margaret Kohl (Minneapolis: Fortress, 2012), 159.

12. Lesslie Newbigin, *The Gospel in a Pluralist Society* (Grand Rapids: Eerdmans, 1989), Kindle edition, location 2010.

13. Rowen Williams, *Relating Intelligently to Religion,* Guardian.com, November 12, 2009, www.theguardian.com/commentisfree/belief /2009/nov/12/faith-development-rowan-williams.

14. Paulo Freire, *Pedagogy of the Oppressed,* trans. Myra Bergman Ramos (New York: Continuum Books, 2003), 7.

15. See Peter Roberts, "Knowledge, Dialogue, and Humanization: Exploring Freire's Philosophy" in Michael Peters, Colin Lankshear, and Mark Olssen, eds., *Critical Theory and the Human Condition: Founders and Praxis* (New York: Peter Lang, 2003), 169–83.

16. Nicholas Wolterstorff, *Educating for Life: Reflections on Christian Teaching and Learning,* ed. Gloria Goris Stronks and Clarence W. Joldersma (Grand Rapids: Baker Academic, 2002), 261.

17. Freire, *Pedagogy,* 73.

18. Robert Putnam, *Bowling Alone: The Collapse and Revival of American Community* (New York: Simon and Schuster, 2001), Kindle edition, location 152.

19. Revelation 21:4, KJV, and Isaiah 28:29, KJV.

20. Revelation 21:4.

21. From that day, 99 percent of her skin graft surgeries were successful. She is married today with two beautiful children.

22. Jürgen Moltmann, Twitter post, August 11, 2012, https://twitter.com /moltmannjuergen/status/234478585472229377.

a word after: all things

1. Frederick Buechner, *Telling Secrets: A Memoir* (New York: HarperCollins, 2009), 92.

2. Matthew 19:25–26.

3. R. T. France, *The Gospel of Matthew,* New International Commentary on the New Testament (Grand Rapids: Eerdmans, 2007), 739.

4. From an interview by World Relief staff in Rwanda on September 26, 2014.

5. Emily Dickinson, *The Poems of Emily Dickinson,* ed. R. W. Franklin (Cambridge, MA: Harvard University Press, 1999), 466.

6. Job 5:16.

7. Frederick Buechner, *Listening to Your Life* (San Francisco: HarperSan-Francisco, 1992), 273–74.

appendix A: the beautiful tree

1. This model is adapted and enhanced from Darrow Miller, *Discipling Nations: The Power of Truth to Transform Cultures* (Seattle, WA: YWAM Publishing, 2011).

2. Luke 6:43, 45, TNIV.

3. Based on Paul Hiebert's theory of worldview, where worldview consists of cognitive (intellectual), affective (emotional), and evaluative (will) dimensions. See Paul Hiebert, *Transforming Worldviews: An Anthropological Understanding of How People Change* (Grand Rapids: Baker Academic, 2008).

4. Hiebert, *Transforming Worldviews,* Kindle edition, location 501.

appendix B: mapping a better future

1. John Kretzmann and John McKnight, *Building Communities from the Inside Out* (Skokie, IL: ACTA Publications, 1993), 8.

2. Diane Dorfman, *Mapping Community Assets Workbook* (Evanston, IL: Northwestern Regional Educational Laboratory, Rural Education Program, 1998), www.abcdinstitute.org/toolkit/.

acknowledgments

While I may have put pen to paper, truth be told, hundreds wrote this book. I am indebted to countless friends, colleagues, and students for shaping my life.

To my colleagues and friends at World Relief and the Justice Conference and, before that, World Hope International and Mercy Ships: your zeal, passion, and love have shaped anything of worth contained herein. A special thanks to the World Relief leadership: Kevin Sanderson, Eeva Simard, John Gichinga, Barry Howard, Dan Kosten, Jenny Yang, Gil Odendaal, Rose Corazza, Lilian Samaan, and James Misner.

Thank you, Bill Haley and Coracle, the Falls Church, and our good friends at St. Brendan's in the City—Andy and Sunita Groth especially—for always caring and always challenging.

Thank you, Tom and Alice Flaherty and City Church, for calling us your own and letting us still call you home.

Thank you, Josh and Rhonda Moody, for taking our sons as your own during our relentless travels.

Thanks to all my friends and colleagues at large, those fighting injustice from so many vantage points: Nicholas and Elsie Hitimana, Gabriel and Jeanette Salguero, Max and Kate Finberg, Lisa Sharon Harper, Inge-Lisa Titheridge, Fiona Hopkins, Dan Browne, Peter Greer, Jeanette Yep, Ken Wytsma, Rob Gailey, Joshua Dubois, Jamie Gates, Justin Dillon, Scott Todd, Michael Wear, Chad Hayward, Noel Costellanos, Galen Carey,

Andy Ryskamp, Matthew Frost, Peter Howard, the Welker family, Jeff and Drew Thomas, "the Wildmans (!)," and the Broses.

To our countless mentors, whether from a distance or close up: John and Susan Yates, Cyprien and Zeburia Nkiriyumwami, Chuck and Sue Duby, Don and Deyon Stephens, Bill and Lynne Hybels, Wayne and Jo Anne Lyon, Warren and Donna Heckman, Bob and Simonne Dyer, Erik and Jeltje Spruyt, Oscar Muriu, Jim Wallis, Tim and Michele Breene, Gary Haugen, Dean and Michelle Sherman, Amb. Tony Hall, Scott and Jewel Arbieter, Susan and Gary Parker, Jack and Cherie Minton, Peter and Karen Schulze, Duane and Muriel Elmer, Tim and Teri Traudt, Mark and Kathy Vaselkiv, Greg and Kit Elmer, Dr. Dave and Susanne Thomas, Steve and Denise Simms, Paul Borhwick, Peter and Linda Warren, Steve and Marie Good, Joel and Becky Hunter, Adm. Tim and Jodi Ziemer, Jean Paul and Clementine Ndagijimana, David Beckmann, Alec Hill at InterVarsity, Evvy Campbell, Robert Gallagher, and Scott Moreau at Wheaton College, Dr. Grace Goodell at Johns Hopkins, and Jason Poling, David Neff, Scott Buresh, members of the illustrious book club to which I belong.

To Brian Fikkert, Russ Mask, Steve Corbett, and the Chalmers gang: thank you for your inspiration and friendship and for writing a book that got so many people thinking.

To those whose writings have framed my own: Miroslav Volf, Jayakumar Christian, Ron Sider, Walter Brueggemann, Nicholas Wolterstorff, Jürgen Moltmann, and so many others already on the other side.

To those who have carved rivers into my soul through image, lyric, and prose: Josh Garrels, Paula Kirby, Trevor Mikula, Jerod Wanner, Ian and Carolyn Christmann, Natalie Salminen, Katie Breckon, Kristy Layton, and so many others.

To Micah Bournes, for your unbridled passion and love for God, his people, and his radical promise and for your silver tongue, which cuts deeply and heals quickly.

To all those who daily endure under injustice: I am your student. Thank you for teaching me.

To three billboards of unconditional love, the friends who know me best: David Lippiatt, Jon Stevens, and Jonathan Ulma.

To my sisters, Rita, Pam, and Brenda (selah), and my in-laws, Phil, Donna, Chris, and Phil, for loving me in spite of.

To my mother, Carolyn Bauman, for listening to that dream in 1959 and pouring out your soul on a tired world.

To my father, James Bauman, for your example and the surety of your word in a flimsy world.

To my wife, Belinda, and my sons, Joshua and Caleb: your joy and tears are spilled here too, mingled with mine.

And to my God, who still capsizes my life only to turn it right-side up again: *Soli Deo gloria.*

about the author

Stephan Bauman is president and CEO of World Relief, an international relief and development organization that serves more than five million vulnerable people each year through more than one hundred thousand church-based volunteers. Stephan's pursuit of justice led him to transition from a successful career in the Fortune 100 sector to Africa, where he directed relief and development programs for nearly a decade before returning to the United States to lead World Relief's global operations. Stephan lives to see people everywhere rise to the call of justice and give their lives in ways that empower the poor toward real change, a journey he continues to pursue. Stephan holds degrees from Johns Hopkins University, Wheaton College, and the University of Wisconsin. He is a poet, an author, an ordained minister, and a certified public accountant. He considers his African friends his most important teachers and his wife, Belinda, his most important mentor. Stephan, Belinda, and their two sons, Joshua and Caleb, live near Washington, DC, and enjoy the woods, the arts, and late-night conversations with friends.